The Holy Rosary through the Visions
of Venerable Mary of Agreda

The

Holy Rosary

Through the Visions of Venerable Mary of Agreda

FR. MARK HIGGINS

CATHOLIC WAY
PUBLISHING

Published in 2022 by Catholic Way Publishing.
Cover & Book design by Catholic Way Publishing.

Compiled and edited by Fr. Mark Higgins. Based on the text: *"Mística Ciudad de Dios"* by Venerable María de Jesús de Ágreda, 1602-1665. English translation: *"Mystical City of God"* by Venerable Mary of Jesus of Ágreda O.I.C., 1914. Translated from the original Spanish by Fiscar Marison (Rev. George J. Blatter).

Illustrations used in this book are works in the public domain. Front Cover Painting: *"Venerable Mary of Agreda"* located at the Embassy of Spain to the Holy See. Oil, Anonymous, 17th century.

This work is published for the greater glory of Jesus Christ through His most holy mother Mary and for the sanctification of the Church militant.

Ordering Information:
Orders by trade bookstores and wholesalers.
Please contact Ingram Content at www.ingramcontent.com.

ISBN-13: 978-1-78379-536-9 (PAPERBACK)
ISBN-13: 978-1-78379-537-6 (HARDBACK)
ISBN-13: 978-1-78379-538-3 (KINDLE E-BOOK)
ISBN-13: 978-1-78379-539-0 (EPUB E-BOOK)

10 9 8 7 6 5 4 3 2 1

Available in E-Book.
www.catholicwaypublishing.com
London, England, UK
2022

"Behold the handmaid of the Lord, be it done to me according to your word."

—THE BLESSED VIRGIN MARY, THE ANNUNCIATION

Contents

The Sorrowful Mysteries

67

The Glorious Mysteries

127

The Mysteries of Light

The Hopeful Mysteries

Introduction

N THE HISTORY OF Our Holy Church, Almighty God has raised up choice daughters; maidens consecrated to His service, and to some, He has whispered into their ears, disclosing to them secrets concerning salvation history, the Life of Christ and the interior life of Our Blessed Mother. Venerable Mary of Jesus of Agreda was one of these privileged souls, who, under strict obedience has left behind to our fallen world a marvellous record of her mystical discoveries, her insights, which are recorded in the lengthy work, 'The Mystical City of God'. It is a collection of books that covers many hundreds of pages, with levels of detail, especially concerning the interior life of Our Lady, which are completely unparalleled in the works of authentic and approved Catholic Mysticism. For many years I hesitated in attempting a worthy presentation of the saint's writings into a format ordered to pious recitation of the Holy Rosary. Surely, I now repent of such a delay, but let me add to this confession that my hesitation was not from sloth or indifference, but rather, from a dizzying awe which came from gazing nervously into the ponderously deep spiritual ocean which is The Mystical City of God.

This compilation of rosary meditations has attempted, possibly for the first time, to abridge this widely acclaimed spiritual classic into a format suited to contemplation of the mysteries of the Holy Rosary. It has done so by ascribing a given text from The Mystical City to each one the beads of the sacred Marian Psalter. This was, however, no mere 'cut and paste' job, far from it, but rather, a lengthy exercise in careful editing, enveloped in prayer. At times, clauses of the saint's writings were necessarily omitted, at other points, lengthy sections condensed or brought together. Such decisions were taken with great apprehensiveness, but necessarily so, in order to ensure that this work can actually be used as a Rosary Companion, with discreet points for short meditation rather than meandering and highly detailed prose.

Venerable Mary of Agreda lived in the Seventeenth Century, and although she lived in a Spain that had already passed its imperial height, it was a Spain, that, spiritually speaking was the jewel in the crown of the remnants of Christendom. In place of the poisonous weeds of protestantism, Spain, in the previous century, had been richly cultivated through the reforming governance of Cisneros, the missionary zeal of Ignatius, the holiness of John and Teresa and the pious rule of Philip II. The influence of these great figures, to their eternal reward, produced a Spain, which, in the century that followed, lived and breathed its Catholic faith. And so, Mary of Agreda entered this world into a deeply Catholic ambience, both on the broader cultural level, but also in the familial, for her parents cherished the holy faith and faithfully formed a home upon this sure foundation. Mary, as a young girl, indeed, a girl almost of the age of Our Lady when she entered the temple, heard the call to religious life, and naturally so, for the quiet voice of Our Lord was more easily perceived and responded to within such a pious environ. This little girl, who was both gifted with intelligence and a certain vivaciousness of spirit, endeavoured to respond to that call as soon as providence permitted. At the age of 12, when Mary finally persuaded her parents to allow her to be admitted to the Discalced Carmelites, Almighty God displayed a rather singular intervention which, although it did not as such change her vocational plans, altered her destination. Mary's holy mother, Catalina, was privileged to received a vision from God just a few days before Mary's entry into Carmel. Our Lord instructed Catalina to convert the family home into a convent, for it to be handed over to the Conceptionist Order, and for all the females in the family to remain in this new community of strict observance. By divine decree, the Spiritual Director of the family, a Franciscan, received the same vision simultaneously, thus confirming the revelation received by Catalina. And so, joyful in this revelation of providence and the Holy Will of God, Ven. Mary, along with her mother, sister and other relations assumed the holy habit, doing so under obedience to mature and seasoned sisters who arrived from Madrid. Under the supervision and guidance of these holy nuns, the new Conceptionist community excelled in religious practice and became renowned for the holiness and zeal of its sisters. Venerable Mary's father, who was still alive, entered the Franciscans as a lay brother, joining the community in which the only two surviving sons of the family had previously entered. At the tender age of 25 Venerable Mary was elected to the role of Abbess of the community, persevering in this holy task for 35 years. As a superior, Mary was prudent, efficient, affectionate and humble. She lived the rule of the order without defect, and, simultaneously, allowed the rule to direct her spiritual maturity, fostering the heights of mysticism even to the Transforming Union. Venerable Mary is justly compared with St. Teresa of Avila, and, whilst Mary never left the convent enclosure, her mystical travels to mission territory through bilocation carry similarities to the tiring apostolic journeys of La Santa. Indeed, Ven. Mary is as much known today for her missionary journeys through bilocation to the southern regions of the now USA (New Mexico, Arizona, Texas), as she is for her Mystical City, to which this work is dedicated. These two facets of her life are not, however, disjoined from each other, because some of the greatest missionaries to the New World, including Blessed Junipero Serra and Ven. Carabantes, were inspired through reading the Mystical City and carried it with them as they undertook their own apostolic labours. Let it be hoped that those who meditate deeply upon the words of the Mystical City, as they pray devoutly the Holy Rosary, will, in our day, be in like manner inspired to spend themselves for the salvation of souls. True and fruitful missionary work always flows from a deep interior life, and, whether you labour domestically in the lay apostolate through organisations like the Legion of Mary, or indeed, offer your life to sow in foreign fields, success, according to the unfailing operations of grace, will only come from this single source. The family home too, the scene of the evangelisation of a new generation of Catholics, and of the guests who enter within its confines, will only produce fruits of holiness and perseverance to the extent that the interior life of its members is assiduously cultivated. Grant, Almighty God, that the Catholics of our lukewarm age may resolutely travel this Way of Perfection, and indeed, that this little work may, in some way, assist them in their holy struggle.

As in previous editions within this series, I have included additional meditations both for the Mysteries of Light, proposed by St. John Paul II, and also the Hopeful Mysteries, a set which concerns events prior to the Annunciation. Our Saint herself would, undoubtedly, be singularly delighted in the inclusion of the Hopeful Mysteries to this work, I say this because, essentially, the Hopeful Mysteries have at their core two elements that were of deep significance to Venerable Mary; the Franciscan view of the Incarnation, and, secondarily, the hidden life of Our Lady.

The Hopeful Mysteries, a purely private devotion, but one which, to Our Lady's delight, grows in knowledge and popularity with each passing day, have been defined as; The Creation of all things in view of Christ, The prophecy of the Redeemer and the Co-Redemptrix, The Birth of the Immaculate Virgin, The Presentation of Mary in the Temple and the Chaste Espousals of Mary and Joseph. Clearly, one can see that these events obviously draw greatly from Our Lady's hidden life, but, moreover, they are deeply 'Franciscan' in a way that especially accords with the spiritual teaching of this holy religious sister.

From her earliest years, Mary of Agreda received, through mystical conferences with heaven, certain insights into the Incarnation of Christ and the predestination of the Immaculate Virgin, understanding these truths as theological facts prior to the foreseeing of Original Sin. Indeed, her understanding and defence of the Immaculate Conception was grounded in this perspective; that Our Lady and her graced conception belong to a decree logically prior in the Mind of God to those decrees concerning the Redemption, which followed logically dependent upon the foreseeing of the Fall. Whilst this perspective is still not dogmatically defined to this day, it is, most evidently, supported by the Catechism of the Catholic Church, and, moreover, echoes the conviction of many of the Church Fathers who pondered deeply upon this mystery. In the years following our saint, during the era in which the heresies of Modernism and Liberalism most violently attacked the Church both from within and without, support for this Franciscan, or Scotist, perspective was more cautiously considered by the Holy See; an approach clearly intended to safeguard the deposit of faith from malicious attack. Unfortunately, however, it was Ven. Mary's support for 'Franciscan' theological positions, or rather, her alleged heavenly imprimatur on these positions, which held Ven. Mary's beatification process, and which has prevented her from being raised to the altars even to this day. Following the beatification of Blessed John Duns Scotus by Pope Benedict XVI, a saint who endured similar caution for like reasons, there is great optimism that, in our age, we may see Venerable Mary rightly acknowledged as a heavenly intercessor and as a virginal companion of the lamb in His glory.

I commend this compilation of rosary mysteries to you, in the hope, as outlined above, that a deep immersion and union in the spirituality of Venerable Mary of Agreda will both elevate you in degrees of grace, but also, and consequently, foster a new impetus in your efforts at evangelisation. The grains of sand pass through the hour glass so rapidly, and in a short time we are old or, failing that, we are infirm, and with a nearness to eternity that we become consciously aware of, even if, sadly, we seem inhibited from mentioning out loud. When, at one time, the age of 30 seemed a milestone nigh unreachable, soon 80 is but a breath away. And for all this, and in all this time, what souls have we brought to God? Souls, the only currency that is of value in the judgement scales of eternity. O Blessed Mother, let my humble recitation of your Holy Rosary merit the graces that I have failed to earn for so much of my useless life, and the scandalously few souls to whom I can claim to have been a real conduit of sanctification and conversion. O Holy Virgin, allow me to drift into a more perfect union with your spirit, so that, when, sooner than I expect, I am plunged into eternity, I may find that at least my own soul, poor though it may be, bears the precious cargo of divine grace, the only hope, the treasure that cannot be stolen.

Yours, in the Immaculate Heart of Mary, Refuge of Sinners,
FR MARK HIGGINS

The Feast of St. Simon Stock, 2022
FRMARKHIGGINS@GMAIL.COM

NOTE ON PRAYING THE ROSARY USING THIS BOOK

If you are praying the rosary alone, it is suggested that you read the initial text before commencing the Our Father. Afterwards, the ten paragraphs of additional meditation can either be read before or during each Hail Mary. In a group setting a leader is required to read aloud each paragraph and commence each Hail Mary. The experience of the editor is that, in private use, with a prayerful silent reading of each passage, to say five mysteries will take at least 4O minutes and for some people closer to 6o. If you feel the movements of grace pulling you into a simpler contemplation of a mystery as you read a paragraph, do not resist the Holy Spirit, and allow yourself to be at rest in the affect (the response of the heart) which Almighty God is stirring from within your soul.

It is customary to commence the Holy Rosary with the Sign of the cross, the apostles Creed, and then, for the intentions of the Holy Father, an Our Father, a Hail Mary, and a Glory Be. After completing five mysteries we then say some concluding prayers centred around the Hail Holy Queen, these are contained at the end of each decade.

The Joyful Mysteries

The Annunciation

THE FRUIT OF THIS MYSTERY

Interior recollection to the presence of God and His holy angels

T THE MOMENT IN which the only begotten of the Father descended to her virginal womb, all the heavens and all creatures were set in commotion. And with the Lord their God, all the hosts of the celestial army issued from heaven, full of invincible strength and splendour. All the material heavens showed deference to their Creator and opened up and parted, as it were, for His passage; the stars shone with greater brilliancy, the moon and sun with the planets hastened their course in the service of their Maker, anxious to witness the greatest of His wonderful works. Mortals did not perceive this commotion and renewal of all the creatures; both because it happened during the night, as well as because the Lord wished it to be known only to the angels. However, in the hearts of some of the just the Most High infused at that hour a new feeling and affection of extraordinary joy of which they became conscious. The birds moved about with new songs and joyousness; the plants and trees gave forth more fruit and fragrance; and in like proportion all the rest of the creatures received and felt some kind of vivifying change. Only for hell it was a cause of new consternation and grief; for at the descent of the Eternal Word from on high, the demons felt an impetuous force of the divine power, which came upon them like the waves of the sea and buried all of them in the deepest caverns of their darkness without leaving them any strength of resistance or recovery. When by divine permission they were again able to rise, they poured forth upon the world and hastened about to discover what strange happening had thus undone them. However, although they held several conferences among themselves, they were unable to find the cause. The Divine Power concealed from them the sacrament of the Incarnation and the manner in which most holy Mary conceived the Incarnate Word. Not until the death of Christ on the cross did they arrive at the certainty that He was true God and true man.

OUR FATHER   Our Father, Who art in Heaven, hallowed be Thy name, Thy kingdom come, Thy will be done, on earth as it is in heaven. Give us this day our daily bread; and forgive us our trespasses, as we forgive those who trespass against us; and lead us not into temptation, but deliver us from evil. Amen.

HAIL MARY (10)   Hail Mary, Full of Grace, the Lord is with thee. Blessed art thou among women and blessed is the fruit of thy womb, Jesus. Holy Mary, mother of God, pray for us sinners now, and at the hour of our death. Amen.

1. I saw that the Eternal Word had awaited and chosen, as the most opportune time and hour for His descent from the bosom of the Father, the midnight of mortal perversion, when the whole posterity of Adam was buried and absorbed in the sleep of forgetfulness and ignorance of their true God. There was nearly no one on earth who opened his mouth in confessing and blessing Him, except some chosen souls among His people. All the rest of the world was lost in silent darkness, having passed a protracted night of thousands of years. Age had succeeded age, and generations followed upon generations, and yet all had Him so near to them, for He had given them life, movement and maintained their very existence.

2. Now the fullness of time had come, for the moment had waited upon the maturity of the most holy Mary, by whose will and consent the Eternal Word would be made flesh. Before all ages this mystery was prearranged in such a way, that it should be fulfilled through the mediation of this heavenly maiden. Now she existed in the world the Redemption of man and the coming of the Only Begotten

of the Father was no longer to be delayed. In order to proceed with a dignity befitting Himself, God prepared most holy Mary in a singular manner during the nine days immediately preceding the Mystery of the Incarnation, and allowed the river of His Divinity to rush impetuously forth to inundate this City of God with Its floods. The Almighty communicated such great graces and gifts and favours to Our Lady at that time; the tongue, the pen, and all the faculties of a creature fall far below any possibility of revealing such incomprehensible wonders.

3. At the bidding of the divine will the holy Gabriel presented himself at the foot of the throne of the Most High. His Majesty then expressly charged him with the message, which he was to bring to the most holy Mary and instructed him in the very words with which he was to salute and address her. Thus the first Author of the message was God Himself, who formed the exact words in His divine mind, and revealed them to the holy archangel for transmission to the most pure Mary. At the same time the Lord revealed to the holy prince Gabriel many hidden wonders concerning the Incarnation. The Blessed Trinity commanded him to betake himself to the heavenly maiden and announce to her, that the Lord had chosen her among women to be the mother of the Eternal Word, that she should conceive Him in her virginal womb through operation of the Holy Spirit without injury to her virginity. In this and in all the rest of the message, which he was to declare and manifest to this great Queen and mistress, the archangel was instructed by the Blessed Trinity Itself. Thereupon His Majesty announced to all the other angels that the time of the Redemption had

come and that He had commanded it to be brought to the world without delay; for already, in their own presence, the most holy Mary had been prepared and adorned to be His mother, and had been exalted to the supreme dignity. The heavenly spirits heard the voice of their Creator, and with incomparable joy and thanksgiving for the fulfilment of His eternal and perfect will, they intoned new canticles of praise, repeating therein that hymn of Sion, "Holy, holy, holy are you, God and Lord of Hosts. Admirable are all Your works, most high and exalted Your designs."

4. The supernal prince Gabriel, obeying with singular delight the divine command and accompanied by many thousands of most beautiful angels in visible forms, descended from the highest heaven. The appearance of the great prince and legate was that of a most handsome youth of rarest beauty; his face emitted resplendent rays of light, his bearing was grave and majestic, his advance measured, his motions composed, his words weighty and powerful, his whole presence displayed a pleasing, kindly gravity and more of godlike qualities than all the other angels until then seen in visible form by the heavenly mistress. He wore a diadem of exquisite splendour and his vestments glowed in various colours full of refulgent beauty. Encased on his breast, he bore a most beautiful cross, disclosing the Mystery of the Incarnation, which he had come to announce. All these circumstances were calculated to rivet the affectionate attention of the most prudent queen. The whole of this celestial army with their princely leader holy Gabriel directed their flight to Nazareth, a town of the province of Galilee, to the dwelling place of most holy Mary. This was a humble cottage and her

chamber was a narrow room, bare of all those furnishings which are generally used by the world in order to hide its own meanness and want of all higher goods. The heavenly mistress was at this time fourteen years, six months and seventeen days of age; for her birthday fell on the eighth of September and six months seventeen days had passed since that date, when this greatest of all mysteries ever performed by God in this world, was enacted in her.

5. At the time when, without her noticing it, the embassy of heaven drew near to her, she was engaged in the highest contemplation concerning the mysteries which the Lord had renewed in her by so many favours during the nine preceding days. And since the Lord Himself had assured her that His Only Begotten would soon descend to assume human form, this great Queen was full of fervent and joyful affection in the expectation of its execution and inflamed with humble love. She spoke in her heart, "Is it possible that the blessed time has arrived, in which the Word of the Eternal Father is to be born and to converse with men? That the world should possess Him? That men are to see Him in the flesh? That His inaccessible light is to shine forth to illumine those who sit in darkness? O, who shall be worthy to see and know Him! O, who shall be allowed to kiss the earth touched by His feet! Rejoice, O you heavens, and console yourself, O earth let all things bless and extol Him, since already His eternal happiness is near! O children of Adam, afflicted with sin, and yet creatures of my Beloved, now shall you raise your heads and throw off the yoke of your ancient servitude! O, O you ancient Forefathers and Prophets, and all you just, that are detained in Limbo and

are waiting in the bosom of Abraham, now shall you be consoled for your much desired and long promised Redeemer is to delay no longer!" In these petitions and aspirations, and in many more too deep for my tongue to explain, the most holy Mary was engaged at the hour when the holy angel Gabriel arrived.

6. The holy Archangel Gabriel, accompanied by innumerable angels in visible human forms and resplendent with incomparable beauty, entered into the chamber where most holy Mary was praying. It was on a Thursday at six o'clock in the evening and at the approach of night. The great modesty and restraint of the princess of heaven did not permit her to look at him more than was necessary to recognise him as an angel of the Lord. Recognising him as such, she, in her usual humility, wished to do him reverence; the holy prince would not allow it; on the contrary he himself bowed profoundly as before his Queen and mistress. The holy archangel saluted our and his Queen and said, "Hail, Full of Grace, the Lord is with you, blessed are you among women". Hearing this new salutation of the angel, Mary, this most humble of all creatures, was disturbed, but not confused in mind. She was disturbed from her humility for she thought herself the lowest of creatures, and thus, in her humility, was taken unawares at hearing herself saluted and called "Blessed among women". On account of this perturbance the angel proceeded to explain to her the decree of the Lord, saying, "Do not fear, Mary, for you have found grace before the Lord; behold you shall conceive a son in your womb, and you shall give birth to Him, and you shall

name Him Jesus; He shall be great, and He shall be called Son of the Most High."

7. As Our Lady herself exceeded the angels in wisdom, prudence and in all sanctity, she delayed her response, in order to be able to give it in accordance with the divine will and that it might be worthy of the greatest of all the mysteries and wonders of the divine power. She reflected that upon her answer depended the pledge of the most Blessed Trinity, the fulfilment of His promises and prophecies, the most pleasing and acceptable of all sacrifices, the opening of the gates of paradise, the victory and triumph over hell, the Redemption of all the human race, the satisfaction of the divine justice, the foundation of the new law of grace, the glorification of men, the rejoicing of the angels, and whatever was connected with the Incarnation of the Only Begotten of the Father and His assuming the form of servant in her virginal womb. A great wonder, indeed, and worthy of our admiration, that all these mysteries and whatever others they included, should be entrusted by the Almighty to a humble maiden and made dependent upon her fiat. But befittingly and securely He left them to the wise and strong decision of this courageous woman, since she would consider them with such magnanimity and nobility, that His confidence in her was not misplaced.

8. Therefore this great lady clothed herself in fortitude, and, having conferred with herself and with the heavenly messenger Gabriel about the grandeur of these high and divine wonders, her purest soul was absorbed and elevated in the highest intensity of divine love. By the intensity of

this interior movement, her most pure heart, as it were by natural consequence, was contracted and compressed with such force, that it distilled three drops of her most pure blood, and these, finding their way to the natural place for the act of conception, were formed by the power of the divine and Holy Spirit, into the body of Christ our Lord. Thus the matter, from which the most holy humanity of the Word for our Redemption is composed, was furnished and administered by the most pure heart of Mary and through the sheer force of her true love. At the same moment, with a humility never sufficiently to be extolled, inclining slightly her head and joining her hands, she pronounced these words, which were the beginning of our salvation, "Be it done to me according to your word".

9. At the pronouncing of this "fiat," so sweet to the hearing of God and so fortunate for us, in one instant, four things happened. First, the most holy body of Christ our Lord was formed from the three drops of blood furnished by the heart of most holy Mary. Secondly, the most holy soul of the same Lord was created, just as other souls. Third, the soul and the body were united in order to compose His perfect humanity. Fourth, the Divinity united Itself in the Person of the Word with the humanity, which together became one composite being in hypostatical union; and thus was formed Christ true God and Man, our Lord and Redeemer. This happened in springtime on the twenty-fifth of March, at break or dawning of the day, in the same hour in which our first father Adam was made at the creation of the world. Not only did most holy Mary herself become a heaven, a temple and dwelling place of the Most Holy Trinity, but her

humble cottage and her poor little oratory was consecrated by the Divinity as a new sanctuary of God. The heavenly spirits, who as witnesses of this marvellous transformation were present to contemplate it, magnified the Almighty with ineffable praise and jubilee; in union with this most happy mother, they blessed Him in His name and in the name of the human race, which was ignorant of this the greatest of His benefits and mercies.

10. The most prudent Queen, seeing herself thus in the immediate presence of the Deity and furnished with the plenitude of divine gifts became lost in humility and love, adoring the Lord in His infinite essence in union with the most holy humanity. She gave Him thanks for having favoured her with the dignity of Mother of God and for the favours done to the whole human race. She gave thanks and glory on behalf of all mankind. She offered herself as an acceptable sacrifice in His service, in the rearing up and nourishing of her sweetest son, ready to assist and co-operate in the work of the Redemption; and the Holy Trinity accepted and appointed her as the Coadjutrix in this mystery. She asked for new graces and divine light for this purpose and for directing herself in the worthy ministration of her office as Mother of the Incarnate Word, that she might treat Him with the veneration and magnanimity due to God Himself. But let no one think that the purest mother was thus favoured and so closely united with the humanity and Divinity of her holiest son, only in order to continue to enjoy spiritual delights and pleasures, free from suffering and pain. Not so, for in closest possible imitation of her sweetest son, this lady lived to share both joy and sorrow

with Him; the memory of what she had so vividly been taught concerning the labours and the death of her holiest son, was like a sword piercing her heart. She took upon herself the long vigil of our Redemption and during all this time this mystery was concealed in her bosom without companionship or alleviation from any creatures.

GLORY BE TO THE FATHER   Glory be to the Father, and to the Son, and to the Holy Spirit, as it was in the beginning, is now and ever shall be, world without end. Amen.

THE FATIMA PRAYER   O my Jesus, forgive us our sins, save us from the fires of hell, lead all souls to heaven, especially those in most need of Thy mercy.

The Visitation

Y THE WORDS OF the heavenly messenger most holy Mary had been informed that her cousin Elizabeth, who was held to be sterile, had conceived a son and that she was already in the sixth month of her pregnancy. Afterwards, the Most High revealed to her that Elizabeth's son would be great before the Lord; a Prophet and the Forerunner of the Incarnate Word. On this same occasion the heavenly Queen was informed that it would be agreeable and pleasing to the Lord if she would visit her cousin, in order that both Elizabeth and the child in her womb might be sanctified by the presence of their Redeemer; for His Majesty was anxious to communicate the benefits of His coming into the world and His merits to His Precursor, in order to make of him, as it were, the well seasoned first fruit of His Redemption. Signifying her readiness to fulfil the divine pleasure, Mary spoke to His Majesty and said, "I, the least of Your creatures, give You humble thanks for kindness which You wish to show to your servant Elizabeth and to the son of her womb. If it is according to the promptings of Your condescension, that I serve you in this work, I stand prepared, my Lord, to obey eagerly Your divine mandates." The Most High answered her, "My dove and My beloved, elect among creatures, I wish, that My and your only begotten go to see Elizabeth, in order to free her son from the chains of the first sin and in order that, before the common and ordinary time decreed for other men, his voice and praise may sound up to My ears and that the mysteries of the Incarnation and Redemption may be revealed to his sanctified soul."

OUR FATHER   Our Father, Who art in Heaven, hallowed be Thy name, Thy kingdom come, Thy will be done, on earth as it is in heaven. Give us this day our daily bread; and forgive us our trespasses, as we forgive those who trespass against us; and lead us not into temptation, but deliver us from evil. Amen.

HAIL MARY (10)   Hail Mary, Full of Grace, the Lord is with thee. Blessed art thou among women and blessed is

the fruit of thy womb, Jesus. Holy Mary, mother of God, pray for us sinners now, and at the hour of our death. Amen.

1. As soon as our lady and Queen arose from the ecstasy in which she had conceived the eternal Incarnate Word, she prostrated herself upon the earth and adored Him in her womb. This adoration she continued all her life, repeating acts of adoration whenever she had opportunity; in this she was even more diligent during the nine months of her divine pregnancy. In order to comply entirely with the new duties consequent upon the guarding of this treasure of the Eternal Father in the virginal bridal chamber, she directed all her attention toward frequent and fervent prayer. She was solicitous in sending up many petitions to be able worthily to preserve the heavenly treasure confided to her. On the day following the Incarnation, the thousand guardian angels which attended upon most holy Mary appeared in corporeal form and with profound humility adored their incarnate King in the womb of the mother. Her also they acknowledged anew as their Queen and mistress and rendered her due homage and reverence, saying, "Now, O lady, you are the true Ark of the Covenant, since you contain the Lawgiver Himself and preserve the Manna of heaven, which is our true bread. Receive, O Queen, our congratulations on account of your dignity and happiness, for which we also thank the Most High; since He has befittingly chosen you for His mother and His tabernacle. We offer anew to you our homage and service, and wish to obey you as vassals and servants of the supreme and omnipotent King, Whose mother you are."

2. Sometimes, in order to afford Our Lady sensible relief, innumerable birds would come to visit her by the command of the Lord. As if they were endowed with intellect, they would salute her by their lively movements, and dividing into harmonious choirs, would furnish her with sweetest music, and they would wait for her blessing before again dispersing. This happened in a special manner soon after she had conceived the Divine Word, as if they wished to congratulate her on her dignity in imitation of the angels. The mistress of all creatures on that day spoke to the different kinds of birds and commanded them to remain and praise with her the Creator, in thanksgiving for the creation, and for the existence and beauty given to them and to sing His praises for their conservation. Immediately they obeyed her as their mistress and anew they began to form choirs, singing in sweetest harmony and bowed low to the ground to worship their Creator and honour the mother, who bore Him in her womb. They were accustomed to bring flowers to her in their beaks and place them into her hands, waiting until she should command them to sing or to be silent according to her wishes. How can our cold hearts not fail to be aroused to adoration of Almighty God, when we see such gratitude offered by His irrational creatures? Merely for the slight participation of the Divinity that consists in bare existence, they proclaim His praises without intermission; whereas we men, who are made to the image and likeness of God, furnished with the powers of knowing Him and enjoying Him eternally, forget Him so far as not even to know Him, and instead of serving Him, offend Him!

3. The humble spouse proceeded to ask the consent of saint Joseph for executing the mandate of the Most High, to visit Elizabeth. In her consummate prudence she said nothing of the mysteries surrounding the Incarnation, but simply spoke to him these words, "My lord and spouse, by the divine light it was made known to me, that through condescension of the Most High the prayer of my cousin Elizabeth, the wife of Zechariah, has been heard; she has conceived a son, though she was sterile. Since she has obtained this singular blessing, I hope that through God's infinite bounty, her son will greatly please and glorify the Lord. I think that on this occasion I am under obligation to visit her and converse with her on certain things for her consolation and spiritual encouragement. If this is according to your liking, my master, I will perform it with your permission, for I am entirely subject to your will and pleasure. Consider then what is best for me and command what I am to do." This prudent silence of the most holy Mary, so full of humble subjection, was very agreeable to the Lord; for she showed herself thereby worthy and capable of receiving the deposit of the great wonders of the King. Therefore, and on account or the confidence in his fidelity with which she proceeded, His Majesty disposed the most pure heart of saint Joseph, giving him His divine light to act conformably to His will. This is the reward of the humble, who ask for counsel, that they will find it with certainty and security. It is also the peculiar prerogative of a holy and discreet zeal to be able to give prudent advice to those that ask. Full of this holy counsel saint Joseph answered our Queen, "You know already, my lady and spouse, that my utmost desires are to serve you with all diligence and attention; for I am bound

to have this confidence in your great virtue, that you will not incline toward anything, which is not according to the greater pleasure and glory of the Most High; and this is my belief also in regard to this journey. Lest your making this journey alone and without the company of your husband cause surprise I will gladly go with you and attend to your wants on the way."

4. The most holy Mary thanked her prudent spouse Joseph for his loving solicitude and for his attentive cooperation with the will of God in whatever he knew to be for His service and honour. They both concluded to depart immediately on their visit to the house of saint Elizabeth and prepared without delay the provisions, which consisted merely in a little fruit, bread and a few fish. In addition to these he borrowed a humble beast of burden, in order to carry their provisions and his spouse, the Queen of all creation. Forthwith they departed from Nazareth for Judea. On leaving their poor dwelling the great mistress of the world knelt at the feet of her spouse Joseph and asked his blessing in order to begin the journey in the name of the Lord. The saint was abashed at the rare humility of his spouse, with which he had already been impressed by experience on so many other occasions. He hesitated giving her his benediction; but the meek and sweet persistence of the most holy Mary overcame his objections and he blessed her in the name of the Most High. The heavenly lady raised her eyes and her heart to God, in order to direct her first steps toward the fulfilment of the divine pleasure and willingly bearing along in her womb the Only Begotten of the Father and her own, for the sanctification of John and that of his mother Elizabeth.

5. Our Lady lovingly hastened to accomplish God's most holy will, in procuring without delay the sanctification of the Precursor of the Incarnate Word, who was yet held prisoner in the womb of Elizabeth by the bonds of original sin. This was the purpose and object of this journey. Leaving behind then the house of her father and forgetting her people, the most chaste spouses, Mary and Joseph, pursued their way to the house of Zechariah in mountainous Judea. It was twenty six leagues distant from Nazareth, and the greater part of the way was very rough and broken, unfit for such a delicate and tender maiden. All the convenience at their disposal for the arduous undertaking was a humble beast, on which she began and pursued her journey. Although it was intended solely for her comfort and service, yet Mary, the most humble and unpretentious of all creatures, many times dismounted and asked her spouse saint Joseph to share with her this commodity and to lighten the difficulties of the way by making use of the beast. Her discreet spouse never accepted this offer; and in order to yield somewhat to the solicitations of the heavenly lady, he permitted her now and then to walk with him part of the way, whenever it seemed to him that her delicate strength could sustain the exertion without too great fatigue. But soon he would again ask her, with great modesty and reverence, to accept of this slight alleviation and the celestial Queen would then obey and again proceed on her way seated in the saddle.

6. The most holy Mary and saint Joseph continued on their journey, making good use of every moment. They proceeded alone, without accompaniment of any human creatures; but all the thousand angels, which were set to guard most holy

Mary, attended upon them. Sometimes Our Lady conversed with the angels and, alternately with them, sang divine canticles concerning the different mysteries of the Divinity and the works of Creation and of the Incarnation. Thus ever anew the pure heart of the immaculate lady was inflamed by the ardours of divine love. In all this her spouse saint Joseph contributed his share by maintaining a discreet silence, and by allowing his beloved spouse to pursue the flights of her spirit; for, lost in highest contemplation, he was favoured with some understanding of what was passing within her soul. At other times the two would converse with each other and speak about the salvation of souls and the mercies of the Lord, of the coming of the Redeemer, of the prophecies given to the ancient Fathers concerning Him, and of other mysteries and wonders of the Most High. In the course of the journey, which lasted four days, the two holy pilgrims, Mary and Joseph, exercised not only the virtues which were interior and had God for their immediate object, but also many other outward acts of charity toward their neighbours; for Mary could not remain idle at the sight of want. They did not find the same hospitable treatment at all the inns of the road; for some of the innkeepers, being more rude, treated them with slight consideration in accordance with their natural disposition; others received them with true love inspired by divine grace. But the mother of mercy denied to no one such help as she could administer; and therefore, whenever she could decently do so, she hastened to visit the poor, infirm and afflicted, helping them and consoling them, and curing their sicknesses. Having pursued their journey four days, the most holy Mary and her spouse arrived at the town of Judah, where Zechariah and Elizabeth then lived.

7. When they arrived at the house of Zechariah, the Precursor of Christ had completed the sixth month of his conception in the womb of saint Elizabeth. The body of the child John had already attained a state of great natural perfection; much greater than that of other children, on account of the miracle of his conception by a sterile mother and on account of the intention of the Most High to make him the depositary of greater sanctity than other men. Yet at that time his soul was yet filled with the darkness of sin, which he had contracted in the same way as the other children of Adam, the first and common father of the human race; and as, according to the universal and general law, mortals cannot receive the light of grace before they have issued forth to the light of the sun. Christ our Lord resolved to anticipate the great blessing of baptism in His Prophet and Precursor by conferring the light of His grace and justification upon him six months after his conception by saint Elizabeth, that he might be His worthy Precursor and Herald. At the pronunciation of Our Lady's words of greeting, God looked upon the child in the womb of saint Elizabeth, and gave it perfect use of reason, enlightening it with His divine light, in order that he might prepare himself by foreknowledge for the blessings which he was to receive. Together with this preparation he was sanctified from original sin, made an adopted son of God, and filled with the most abundant graces of the Holy Spirit and with the plenitude of all His gifts; his faculties were sanctified, subjected and subordinated to reason, thus verifying in himself what the Archangel Gabriel had said to Zechariah; that his son would be filled with the Holy Spirit from the womb of His mother. At the same time the fortunate child,

looking through the walls of the maternal womb as through clear glass upon the Incarnate Word, and assuming a kneeling posture, adored his Redeemer and Creator, whom he beheld in most holy Mary as if enclosed in a chamber made of the purest crystal. This was the movement of jubilation, which was felt by his mother Elizabeth as coming from the infant in her womb.

8. Saint Elizabeth was instructed at the same time in the mystery of the Incarnation, the sanctification of her own son and the purpose of this new wonder. She also became aware of the virginal purity and of the dignity of most holy Mary. The efficacious instrument of these graces was the voice of most holy Mary, as powerful as it was sweet. All this force was, as it were, only an outflow of that which was contained in those powerful words, "Be it done to me according to your word", by which she had drawn the Eternal Word from the bosom of the Father down to her soul and into her womb. Filled with admiration at what she saw and heard in regard to these divine mysteries, saint Elizabeth was wrapt in the joy of the Holy Spirit; and, looking upon the Queen of the world and what was contained in her, she burst forth in loud voice of praise, pronouncing the words reported to us by saint Luke. In these prophetic words saint Elizabeth rehearsed the noble privileges of most holy Mary, perceiving by the divine light what the power of the Lord had done in her, what He now performed, and what He was to accomplish through her in time to come. All this also the child John perceived and understood, while listening to the words of his mother; for she was enlightened for the purpose of his sanctification, and since he could not from his place in the

womb bless and thank her by word of mouth, she, both
for herself and for her son, extolled the most holy Mary
as being the instrument of such blessings. These words of
praise, pronounced by saint Elizabeth were referred by the
mother of wisdom and humility to the Creator; and in the
sweetest and softest voice she intoned the Magnificat as
recorded by saint Luke.

9. Our Lady offered to serve and assist Elizabeth as a handmaid, for this, she said, was her purpose of visiting her and
consoling her. O what friendship is so true, so sweet and
inseparable, as that which is formed by the great bond of
the divine love! Having passed a long time in prayerful
retirement with Elizabeth, the Queen returned to the main
part of the house. There she saw Zechariah standing before
her in his muteness, and she asked him for his blessing as
from a priest of the Lord, which the saint also gave to her.
Yet, although she tenderly pitied him for his affliction, she
did not exert her power to cure him, because she knew the
mysterious occasion of his dumbness; yet she offered a prayer
for him. After staying three days in the house of Zechariah,
St. Joseph asked permission of his heavenly spouse Mary to
return to Nazareth and leave her in the company of saint
Elizabeth in order to assist her in her pregnancy. The holy
husband left them with the understanding that he was to
return in order to accompany the Queen home as soon as
they should give him notice; saint Elizabeth offered him
some presents to take home with him; but he would take
only a small part of them, yielding only to their earnest
solicitations, for this man of God was not only a lover of

poverty, but was possessed of a magnanimous and noble heart. Therewith he pursued his way back to Nazareth.

10. From the time of her receiving the Lord as her Guest in her house, though yet in the womb of the Virgin Mother, the holy Elizabeth was much favoured by God. By the continued conversation with the heavenly Queen, in proportion as she grew in the knowledge and understanding of the mysteries of the Incarnation, this great matron advanced in all manner of sanctity, as one who draws it from its very fountain. A few times she merited to see most holy Mary during her prayers, ravished and raised from the ground and altogether filled with divine splendour and beauty, so that she could not have looked upon her face, nor remain alive in her presence, if she had not been strengthened by divine power. On these occasions she prostrated herself most discreetly in Our Lady's presence, adoring the Incarnate Word in the virginal temple of the most holy mother. All the mysteries which became known to her by the divine light and by conversations with the great Queen, saint Elizabeth sealed up in her bosom, being a most faithful depositary and prudent secretary of that which was confided to her. Only with her son John and with Zechariah, during the short time in which he lived after the birth of his son, saint Elizabeth conversed to some extent concerning those wonders which had become known to all. But in all this she acted as a courageous, wise and very holy woman. Most holy Mary, Our Lady, was present not only at the confinement of saint Elizabeth and at the birth of John, but also at the naming and circumcision of saint John. When the Queen of the Universe held the infant John in her arms, she was,

for a short time, secretly wrapt in sweetest ecstasy; during it she offered up a devout prayer for the child, holding him close to the same breast where the Only Begotten of the Eternal, and her own, was soon to rest.

GLORY BE TO THE FATHER   Glory be to the Father, and to the Son, and to the Holy Spirit, as it was in the beginning, is now and ever shall be, world without end. Amen.

THE FATIMA PRAYER   O my Jesus, forgive us our sins, save us from the fires of hell, lead all souls to heaven, especially those in most need of Thy mercy.

The Nativity of Jesus Christ

THE FRUIT OF THIS MYSTERY

Absorption in God during times of Eucharistic Adoration

HE MOST HOLY MARY remained in ecstasy, caught up in the beatific vision for over an hour immediately prior to giving birth. At the moment when she regained the use of her senses she felt and saw that the body of the infant God had begun to move in her womb. Releasing and freeing Himself from the place which He had occupied for nine months, He now prepared to issue forth from that sacred bridal chamber. This movement not only did not cause any pain or hardship, as happens with the other daughters of Adam and Eve in their childbirths; but filled her with incomparable joy and delight, causing in her soul and body such exalted and divine effects that they exceed all thoughts of men. Her body became so spiritualised with the beauty of heaven that she seemed no more a human and earthly creature. Her countenance emitted rays of light, like a sun, she shone in indescribable earnestness and majesty, all inflamed with fervent love. She was kneeling in the manger, her eyes raised to heaven, her hands joined and folded at her breast, her soul wrapped in the Divinity. In this position, and at the end of the heavenly rapture, the most exalted lady gave to the world the Only Begotten of the Father and her own, our Saviour Jesus, true God and man. It was at the hour of midnight, on a Sunday, at the beginning of the 25th of December.

OUR FATHER   Our Father, Who art in Heaven, hallowed be Thy name, Thy kingdom come, Thy will be done, on earth as it is in heaven. Give us this day our daily bread; and forgive us our trespasses, as we forgive those who trespass against us; and lead us not into temptation, but deliver us from evil. Amen.

HAIL MARY (10)   Hail Mary, Full of Grace, the Lord is with thee. Blessed art thou among women and blessed is the fruit of thy womb, Jesus. Holy Mary, mother of God, pray for us sinners now, and at the hour of our death. Amen.

1. It had been decreed by the immutable will of Providence that the Only Begotten of the Father should be born in the

town of Bethlehem. The fulfilment of this immutable decree the Lord secured by means of an edict of Caesar Augustus for the whole Roman empire, ordering the inhabitants to pay a certain tax to their temporal lord, doing so in his native city. Unsure as to whether the Virgin ought to accompany him, St. Joseph asked her to consult the Most High in order to receive instruction. Having conferred with the Lord, the Holy Virgin announced to him that Almighty God willed that she accompany him on his journey to Bethlehem. Joseph was filled with new consolation and delight. They then resolved upon the day of their departure, and Joseph diligently searched in the town of Nazareth for some beast of burden to bear the mistress of the world. He could not easily find one because so many people were going to different towns in order to fulfil the requirements of the edict of the emperor. But after much anxious inquiry saint Joseph found an unpretentious little beast which, if we can call such creatures fortunate, was the most fortunate of all the irrational animals; since it was privileged not only to bear the Queen of all creation and the blessed fruit of her womb, the King of Kings and the Lord of Lords, but afterwards to be present at His Birth; and to give its Creator the homage denied to Him by men. They carried with them bread, fruit and some fishes, which ordinarily composed their nourishment. As the most prudent Virgin was enlightened regarding their protracted absence, she made use of prudent concealment in taking along the linens and clothes necessary for her heavenly delivery, for she wished to dispose all things according to the exalted intents of the Lord and in preparation for the events which she expected. Their house they left in charge of a neighbour until they should return.

2. The most pure Mary and the glorious saint Joseph departed from Nazareth for Bethlehem alone, poor and humble in the eyes of the world. None of the mortals thought more of them than what was warranted by their poverty and humility. But O the wonderful wonders of the Most High, hidden to the proud, and unpenetrated by the wisdom of the flesh! They did not walk alone, poor or despised, but prosperous, rich and in magnificence. They were most worthy of the immense love of the Eternal Father and most estimable in His eyes. They carried with them the treasure of heaven, the Deity itself. The whole court of the celestial ministers venerated them. All the inanimate beings recognised the living and true Ark of the Testament more readily than the waters of the Jordan recognised its type and shadow, when they courteously laid open and free the path for its passage and for those that followed it. They were accompanied by the ten thousand angels, appointed by God Himself as the servants of her Majesty during that whole journey. These heavenly squadrons marched along as their retinue in human forms visible to the heavenly lady, more refulgent than so many suns. The sovereign Queen experienced no darkness of night on the way; for a few times, when their travel extended beyond nightfall the holy angels spread about such effulgence as not all the lights of heaven in their noontide splendour would have thrown forth in the clearest heavens. This light and vision of the angels also saint Joseph enjoyed at those times; then all of them together would form celestial choirs, in which they and the two holy travellers alternated in singing wonderful hymns and canticles of praise, converting the fields into new heavens.

3. With these wonderful favours and delights, however, the Lord joined some hardships and inconveniences, which the divine mother encountered on the way. For the behaviour of people in the inns, occasioned by the imperial edict, was very disagreeable and annoying to the modest and retiring Virgin-mother and her spouse. On account of their poverty and timid retirement they were treated with less hospitality and consideration than others, especially the well-to-do; for the world judges and usually confers its favours according to outward appearance and according to personal influence. Our holy pilgrims were obliged repeatedly to listen to sharp reprimands in the inns, at which they arrived tired out by their journey, and in some of them they were refused admittance as worthless and despicable people. Several times they assigned to the mistress of heaven and earth some corner of the hallway; while at others she did not fare even so well, being obliged to retire with her husband to places still more humble and unbecoming in the estimation of the world. The heavenly lady observed and knew the secrets of the different souls of those she met, penetrating into the very thoughts and conditions of each, whether of grace or of guilt in their different degrees. Concerning many souls she also knew whether they were predestined or reprobate, whether they would persevere, fall, or again rise up. All this variety of insight moved her to the exercise of heroic virtues as well in regard to the ones as to the others. For many of them she obtained the grace of perseverance, for others efficacious help to rise from their sin to grace; for others again she prayed to the Lord with affectionate tears, feeling intensest sorrow for the reprobate, though she did not pray as efficaciously for them. Many times, worn out by

these sorrows, much more than by the hardships of travel, the strength of her body gave way; on such occasions the holy angels, full of refulgent light and beauty, bore her up in their arms, in order that she might rest and recuperate. The sick, afflicted and indigent whom she met on the way, she consoled and assisted by asking her most holy son to come to their aid in their necessities and adversities. She kept herself silently aloof from the multitude, preoccupied with the Fruit of her divine pregnancy, which was already evident to all.

4. Our travellers arrived at the town of Bethlehem at four o'clock of the fifth day, a Saturday. As it was at the time of the winter solstice, the sun was already sinking and the night was falling. They entered the town, and wandered through many streets in search of a lodging-house or inn for staying over night. They knocked at the doors of their acquaintances and nearer family relations; but they were admitted nowhere and in many places they met with harsh words and insults. The most modest Queen followed her spouse through the crowds of people, while he went from house to house and from door to door. Although she knew that the hearts and the houses of men were to be closed to them, and although to expose her state at her age to the public gaze was more painful to her modesty than their failure to procure a night lodging, she nevertheless wished to obey saint Joseph and suffer this indignity and unmerited shame. While wandering through the streets they passed the office of the public registry and they inscribed their names and paid the fiscal tribute in order to comply with the edict and not be obliged to return. They continued their search, betaking

themselves to other houses. But having already applied at more than fifty different places, they found themselves rejected and sent away from them all. The heavenly spirits were filled with astonishment at these exalted mysteries of the Most High, which manifested the patience and meekness of His Virgin Mother and the unfeeling hardness of men. At the same time they blessed the Almighty in His works and hidden wonders, since from that day on He began to exalt and honour poverty and humility among men. It was nine o'clock at night when the most faithful Joseph, full of bitter and heart-rending sorrow, returned to his most prudent spouse and said, "My sweetest lady, my heart is broken with sorrow at the thought of not only not being able to shelter you as you deserve and as I desire, but in not being able to offer you even any kind of protection from the weather, or a place of rest, a thing rarely or never denied to the most poor and despised in the world. No doubt heaven, in thus allowing the hearts of men to be so unmoved as to refuse us a night-lodging, conceals some mystery. I now remember, lady, that outside the city walls there is a cave, which serves as a shelter for shepherds and their flocks. Let us seek it out; perhaps it is unoccupied, and we may there expect some assistance from heaven, since we receive none from men on earth." The most prudent Virgin answered, "My spouse and my master, let not your kindest heart be afflicted because the ardent wishes which the love of your Lord excites in you cannot be fulfilled. Since I bear Him in my womb, let us, I beseech you, give thanks for having disposed events in this way. The place of which you speak shall be most satisfactory to me. Let your tears of sorrow be turned into tears of joy, and let us lovingly embrace poverty,

which is the inestimable and precious treasure of my most
holy son. Let us go gladly wherever the Lord shall guide us."
When they arrived at the city gate they saw that the cave
was forsaken and unoccupied. Full of heavenly consolation,
they thanked the Lord for this favour.

5. The palace which the supreme King of kings and the
Lord of Lords had chosen for entertaining His Eternal and
Incarnate Son in this world was a most poor and insignif-
icant hut or cave, to which most holy Mary and Joseph
betook themselves after they had been denied all hospitality
and the most ordinary kindness by their fellow-men. This
place was held in such contempt that, though the town of
Bethlehem was full of strangers in want of night shelter,
none would demean or degrade himself so far as to make
use of it for a lodging; for there was none who deemed it
suitable or desirable for such a purpose, except the Teachers of humility and poverty, Christ our Saviour and His
purest mother. Most holy Mary and saint Joseph entered
the lodging thus provided for them and by the effulgence
of the ten thousand angels of their guard they could easily
ascertain its poverty and loneliness, which they esteemed
as favours and welcomed with tears of consolation and joy.
Without delay the two holy travellers fell on their knees
and praised the Lord, giving Him thanks for His benefit,
which they knew had been provided by His wisdom for His
own hidden designs. Of this mystery the heavenly princess
Mary had a better insight; for as soon as she sanctified the
interior of the cave by her sacred footsteps she felt a fullness
of joy which entirely elevated and vivified her. She besought
the Lord to bless with a liberal hand all the inhabitants of

the neighbouring city, because by rejecting her they had given occasion to the vast favours, which she awaited in this neglected cavern. It was formed entirely of the bare and coarse rocks, without any natural beauty or artificial adornment; a place intended merely for the shelter of animals; yet the Eternal Father had selected it for the shelter and dwelling-place of His own Son.

6. Having spent a short time in this prayer and conferring about the mysteries of the Incarnate Word, the most prudent Virgin felt the approach of the most blessed Birth. She requested her spouse saint Joseph to betake himself to rest and sleep as the night was already far advanced. The man of God yielded to the request of his spouse and urged her to do the same; and for this purpose he arranged and prepared a sort of couch with the articles of wear in their possession, making use of a crib or manger, that had been left by the shepherds for their animals. Leaving most holy Mary in the portion of the cave thus furnished, saint Joseph retired to a corner of the entrance, where he began to pray. He was immediately visited by the Divine Spirit and felt a most sweet and extraordinary influence, by which he was wrapt and elevated into an ecstasy. In it was shown him all that passed during that night in this blessed cave; for he did not return to consciousness until his heavenly spouse called him. Such was the sleep which saint Joseph enjoyed in that night, more exalted and blessed than that of Adam in paradise.

7. Following a lengthy ecstasy of prayer, and in a rapture of divine love, the Sun of Justice was born; the Only Begotten

of the Eternal Father and of Mary most pure, beautiful, refulgent and immaculate. He left her untouched in her virginal integrity and purity, making her more godlike and forever sacred; passing from her body as the rays of the sun penetrate a crystal, thus He shone, illuminating her in prismatic beauty. The Virgin mother, having brought forth her first begotten son, wrapped Him in swathing clothes and placed Him in a manger. The two sovereign princes, saint Michael and saint Gabriel, were the assistants of the Virgin on this occasion. They stood by at proper distance in human corporeal forms at the moment when the Incarnate Word, penetrating the virginal chamber by divine power, issued forth to the light, and they received Him in their hands with ineffable reverence. In the same manner as a priest exhibits the sacred host to the people for adoration, so these two celestial ministers presented to the divine mother her glorious and refulgent Son. All this happened in a short space of time. In the same moment in which the holy angels thus presented the divine child to His mother, both son and mother looked upon each other, and in this look, she wounded with love the sweet Infant and was at the same time exalted and transformed in Him. From the arms of the holy princes the Prince of all the heavens spoke to His holy mother, "Mother, become like unto Me, since on this day, for the human existence, which you have today given Me, I will give you another more exalted existence in grace, assimilating your existence as a mere creature to the likeness of Me, who am God and Man."

8. After this interchange of words, so full of mysteries, the divine child suspended the miracle of His transfiguration, or

rather He inaugurated the other miracle, that of suspending the effects of glory in His most holy body, confining them solely to His soul; and He now assumed the appearance of one capable of suffering. In this form the most pure mother now saw Him and, still remaining in a kneeling position and adoring Him with profound humility and reverence, she received Him in her arms from the hands of the holy angels. The mother of mercy turned also toward all mortals and addressed them, saying, "Be consoled O you afflicted and rejoice O you disconsolate, be raised up O you fallen, come to rest O you uneasy. Let the just be gladdened and the saints be rejoiced; let the heavenly spirits break out in new jubilee, let the Prophets and Patriarchs of Limbo draw new hope, and let all the generations praise and magnify the Lord, who renews His wonders. Come, come O you poor; approach O you little ones, without fear, for in my arms I bear the lion made a lamb, the Almighty, become weak, the Invincible subdued. Come to draw life, hasten to obtain salvation, approach to gain eternal rest, since I have all this for all, and it will be given to you freely and communicated to you without envy. Do not be slow and heavy of heart, O you sons of men; and You, O sweetest joy of my soul, give me permission to receive from You that kiss desired by all creatures." Therewith the most blessed mother applied her most chaste and heavenly lips in order to receive the loving caresses of the divine child, who on His part, as her true son, had desired them from her.

9. It was now time to call saint Joseph, the faithful spouse of the most discreet and attentive lady. He was wrapped in ecstasy, in which he was informed by divine revelation

of all the mysteries of this sacred birth during this night. But it was becoming that he should see, and, before all other mortals, should in his corporeal faculties and senses be present and experience, adore and reverence the Word made flesh; for he of all others had been chosen to act as the faithful warden of this great sacrament. At the desire of his heavenly spouse he left his ecstasy and, on being restored to consciousness, the first sight of his eyes was the divine child in the arms of the Virgin Mother reclining against her sacred countenance and breast. There he adored Him in profoundest humility and in tears of joy. He kissed His feet in great joy and admiration, which no doubt would have taken away and destroyed life in him, if divine power had not preserved it; and he certainly would have lost all the use of his senses, if the occasion had permitted. When saint Joseph had begun to adore the child, the most prudent mother asked leave of her son to arise (for until then she had remained on her knees) and, while saint Joseph handed her the wrappings and swaddling clothes, which she had brought, she clothed Him with incomparable reverence, devotion and tenderness. Having thus swathed and clothed Him, His mother, with heavenly wisdom, laid Him in the crib. For this purpose she had arranged some straw and hay upon a stone in order to prepare for the God-Man His first resting-place upon earth next to that which He had found in her arms. According to divine ordainment an ox from the neighbouring fields ran up in great haste and, entering the cave, joined the beast of burden brought by the Queen. The blessed mother commanded them, with what show of reverence was possible to them to acknowledge and adore their Creator. The humble animals obeyed their mistress and prostrated themselves before the child, warming Him with their breath and rendering Him the service refused by men.

10. After the courtiers of heaven had celebrated the birth of God made man near the portals of Bethlehem, some of them were immediately dispatched to different places, in order to announce the happy news to those, who according to the divine will were properly disposed to hear it. The holy prince Michael betook himself to the holy Patriarchs in Limbo and announced to them, how the Only Begotten of the Eternal Father was already born into the world and was resting, humble and meek, as they had prophesied, in a manger between two beasts. Another of the holy angels that attended and guarded the heavenly mother was sent to saint Elizabeth and her son John. On hearing this news of the birth of the Redeemer, the prudent matron and her son, although he was yet of so tender an age, prostrated themselves upon the earth and adored their God made man in spirit and in truth. Other angels were delegated to bring the news to Zechariah, Simeon and Anna, the prophetess, and to some other just and holy people, who were worthy to be trusted with this new mystery of our Redemption. Although not all the just upon earth were informed at that time of this mystery; yet in all of them came to pass certain divine effects in the hour in which the Saviour of the world was born. For all the just felt in their hearts a new and supernatural joy, though they were ignorant of its cause. There were not only movements of joy in the angels and in the just, but also wonderful movements in the insensible creatures; for all the influences of the planets were renovated and enlivened. The sun much accelerated its course; the

stars shone in greater brightness; and for the Magi kings was formed that wonderful star, which showed them the way to Bethlehem. Many trees began to bloom and others to produce fruit. Some temples of the idols were overthrown; and in others the idols were hurled down and their demons put to flight. These wonders and other happenings in the world on that day men accounted for in different ways, but far from the truth. Only among the just there were many, who by divine impulse suspected or believed that God had come into the world; yet no one knew it with certainty, except those to whom it was revealed. Among these were the three Magi, to each of whom in their separate Oriental kingdoms angels were sent to inform them by interior and intellectual enlightenment that the Redeemer of the human race had been born in poverty and humility. At the same time they were inspired with the sudden desire of seeking Him and adoring Him, and immediately they saw the star as a guide to Bethlehem.

GLORY BE TO THE FATHER   Glory be to the Father, and to the Son, and to the Holy Spirit, as it was in the beginning, is now and ever shall be, world without end. Amen.

THE FATIMA PRAYER   O my Jesus, forgive us our sins, save us from the fires of hell, lead all souls to heaven, especially those in most need of Thy mercy.

The Purification of Mary and the Presentation of the Infant Christ in the Temple

THE FRUIT OF THIS MYSTERY

To pass unnoticed in this world

IN ORDER TO COMPLY with the law and satisfy the obligation which demanded the sanctification and presentation to the Lord of all the firstborn sons, the mother of all purity prepared to go to Jerusalem, where she was to appear in the temple with her son as the Only Begotten of the Eternal Father and purify herself according to the custom of other women. She had no doubts about complying with the purification, which applied to herself in common with other mothers. Not that she was ignorant of her innocence and purity; for, ever since the Incarnation of the Word, she knew of her exemption from actual sin and from the stain of original sin. Nor was she ignorant of the fact that she had conceived by the Holy Spirit, and brought forth without labour, remaining a virgin more pure than the sun. Yet she hesitated not to subject herself to the common law; on the contrary, in the ardent longing of her heart after humiliation and annihilation to the dust, she desired to do this of her own free will. When the ceremony of the presentation had concluded, the great lady kissed the hand of the priest and again asked his blessing. The same she did also to Anna, her former teacher; for her dignity as Mother of God, the highest possible to angels or men, did not prevent her from these acts of deepest humility. Then, in the company of saint Joseph, her spouse, and of the fourteen thousand angels in procession, she returned with the divine infant to her lodging.

OUR FATHER   Our Father, Who art in Heaven, hallowed be Thy name, Thy kingdom come, Thy will be done, on earth as it is in heaven. Give us this day our daily bread; and forgive us our trespasses, as we forgive those who trespass against us; and lead us not into temptation, but deliver us from evil. Amen.

HAIL MARY (10)   Hail Mary, Full of Grace, the Lord is with thee. Blessed art thou among women and blessed is the fruit of thy womb, Jesus. Holy Mary, mother of God, pray for us sinners now, and at the hour of our death. Amen.

1. The most pure Mary and her spouse, having with her divine child moved to the dwelling in the vicinity of the cave, remained there until, according to the requirements of the law, she was to be present herself with her First-born for purification in the temple. For this mystery the most holy of creatures resolved to dispose herself worthily by a fervent desire of carrying the infant Jesus as an offering to the Eternal Father in His temple; by imitating her son and by seeking the adornment and beauty of great virtues as a worthy offering and victim for the Most High. With this intention the heavenly lady, during the days which still remained until her purification, performed such heroic acts of love and of all other virtues, that neither the tongue of angels nor of men can explain them.

2. During the days in which the most holy Queen stayed near Bethlehem before the purification, some of the people came to see and speak with her; but almost all of them were of the poorest class. Some of them came because of the alms which she distributed, others, because they had heard of the Kings, who had visited the cave. All of them spoke of this visit and of the coming of the Redeemer; for in those days the belief, that the birth of the Messiah was at hand was very widespread among the Jews, and the talk about it was very frequent. This gave the most prudent mother repeated occasion to exercise herself in magnanimous

works, not only by guarding the secret of her bosom and by
conferring within herself about all that she saw and heard,
but also by directing many souls toward the knowledge of
God, by confirming them in the faith, instructing them in
the practice of virtues, enlightening them in the mysteries
of the Messiah whom they were expecting, and dispelling
the ignorance, in which they were cast as a low-minded
people, little versed in the things of God. Sometimes their
talk about these matters was so full of error that the simple
saint Joseph smiled in secret. He wondered at the heavenly
wisdom and force of the answers, with which the great lady
met their gossip and instructed them; at her patience and
gentleness in leading them to the truth and to the perception of the light; at her profound humility and yet patient
reserve, with which she knew how to dismiss all of them
consoled, rejoiced and furnished with all that was good
for them to know. She spoke to them words of eternal life,
which penetrated, inflamed and strengthened their hearts.

3. In regard to the presentation of her most holy son there
was some occasion for the same doubt as in regard to the
Circumcision, for she knew Him to be the true God, superior to the laws, which He Himself had made. But she
was informed of the will of the Lord by divine light and
by the interior acts of the most holy soul of the Incarnate
Word; for she saw His desire of sacrificing Himself and
offering Himself as a living Victim to the Eternal Father, in
thanksgiving for having formed His most pure body and
created His most holy soul; for having destined Him as an
acceptable sacrifice for the human race and for the welfare
of mortals. He wished to be offered to the Eternal Father

in the temple where all adored and magnified Him, as in a house of prayer, expiation and sacrifice.

4. The great lady conferred about the journey with her husband, and, having resolved to be in Jerusalem on the very day appointed by the law and having made the necessary preparations, they took leave of the good woman in whose house they had been staying and who had so devotedly taken care of them. Although this woman was left in ignorance of the divine mysteries connected with her guests, she was filled with the blessings of heaven, which brought her abundant fruit. Mary and Joseph betook themselves to the cave of the Nativity, not wishing to begin their journey without once more venerating that sanctuary so humble and yet so rich in happiness, though at that time this was yet unknown to the world. The mother handed the child Jesus to saint Joseph in order to prostrate herself and worship the earth which had been witness to such venerable mysteries. She covered herself with a cloak for the journey and, receiving in her arms Jesus, the treasure of heaven, she pressed Him to her breast, tenderly shielding Him from the inclemency of the wintry weather. They departed from the cave, asking the blessing of the infant God, which His Majesty gave them in a visible manner. Saint Joseph placed upon the ass the chest containing the clothes of the Infant and the gifts of the Kings destined for their temple-offering. Thus began the most solemn procession, which was ever held from Bethlehem to the temple in Jerusalem.

5. During the journey of our lady with the infant God, it happened in Jerusalem that Simeon, the high priest, was

enlightened by the Holy Spirit concerning the coming of the Incarnate Word and His presentation in the temple on the arms of His mother. The same revelation was given to the holy widow Anna, and she was also informed of the poverty and suffering of saint Joseph and the most pure lady on their way to Jerusalem. These two holy persons, immediately conferring with each other about their revelations and enlightenments, called the chief procurator of the temporal affairs of the temple, and, describing to him the signs, whereby he should recognise the holy travellers, they ordered him to proceed to the gate leading out to Bethlehem and receive them into his house with all benevolence and hospitality. This the procurator did and thus the Queen and her spouse were much relieved, since they had been anxious about finding a proper lodging for the divine Infant. Leaving them well provided in his house, the fortunate host returned in order to report to the high priest.

6. On that evening, before they retired, most holy Mary and Joseph conferred with each other about what they were to do. The most prudent lady reminded him that it was better to bring the gifts of the Kings on that same evening to the temple in order to be able to make the offering in silence and without noisy demonstration, as was proper with all donations and sacrifices, and that on the way he might procure the two turtle-doves, which on the next day were to be the public offering for the Infant Jesus. Saint Joseph complied with her request. As a stranger and one little known he gave the myrrh, incense and gold to the one who usually received such gifts for the temple, but saint Joseph took care not to reveal himself to anyone as

the donor of these great presents. Although he could have bought the lamb, which the rich usually offered for their first-born, he chose not to do so; because the humble and poor apparel of the mother and the child as well as of the husband, would not have agreed with a public offering as valuable as that of the rich. In no particular did the mother of wisdom deem it befitting to depart from poverty and humility, even under the cover of a pious and honourable intention. For in all things was she the teacher of perfection, and her most holy son, that of holy poverty, in which He was born, lived and died.

7. Simeon was a just and god-fearing man and was hoping in the consolation of Israel; the Holy Spirit, who dwelt in him, had revealed to him that he should not taste death until he had seen the Christ, the Lord. Moved by the Holy Spirit he came to the temple; for in that night, besides the revelations he had already received, he was again divinely enlightened and made to understand more clearly the mysteries of the Incarnation and Redemption of man, the fulfilment of the prophecies of Isaiah, that a Virgin should conceive and bear a son and that from the root of Jesse a flower should blossom, namely Christ; likewise all the rest contained in these and other prophecies. He received a clear understanding of the hypostatic union of the two natures in the person of the Word, and of the mysteries of the passion and death of the Redeemer. Thus instructed in these two high things, saint Simeon was lifted up and inflamed with the desire of seeing the Redeemer of the world. On the following day then, as soon as he had received notice that Christ was coming to present Himself in the temple to the

Father, he was carried in spirit to the temple, for so great is the force of divine enlightenment. Also the holy matron Anna was favoured with a revelation during the same night concerning many of these mysteries and great was the joy of her spirit on that account.

8. On the next morning, the Sun of Heaven being now ready to issue from its purest dawning, the Virgin Mary, on whose arms He reclined, and being about to rise up in full view of the world, the heavenly lady, having provided the turtle-dove and two candles, wrapped Him in swaddling-clothes and betook herself with saint Joseph from their lodging to the temple. Having arrived at the temple-gate, the most blessed mother was filled with new and exalted sentiments of devotion. Joining the other women, she bowed and knelt to adore the Lord in spirit and in truth in His holy temple and she presented herself before the exalted Majesty of God with His Son upon her arms. Immediately she was immersed in an intellectual vision of the Most Holy Trinity and she heard a voice issuing from the Eternal Father, saying, "This is My beloved Son, in whom I am well pleased". Saint Joseph, the most fortunate of men, felt at the same time a new sweetness of the Holy Spirit, which filled him with joy and divine light.

9. The holy high-priest Simeon, moved by the Holy Spirit also entered the temple at that time. Approaching the place where the Queen stood with the Infant Jesus in her arms, he saw both mother and child enveloped in splendour and glory. The prophetess Anna, who had come at the same hour, also saw Mary and her Infant surrounded by this wonderful

light. In the joy of their spirit both of them approached the Queen of heaven, and the priest received the Infant Jesus from her arms upon his hands. Raising up his eyes to heaven he offered Him up to the Eternal Father, pronouncing at the same time these words so full of mysteries, "Now You may dismiss Your servant, O Lord, according to Your Word in peace. Because my eyes have seen your salvation, which You have prepared before the face of all peoples, a light for the revelation of the gentiles, and the glory of your people Israel". It was as if he had said, "Now, Lord, You will release me from the bondage of this mortal body and let me go free and in peace; for until now have I been detained in it by the hope of seeing your promises fulfilled and by the desire of seeing Your Only Begotten made man. Now that my eyes have seen Your salvation, the Only Begotten made man, joined to our nature in order to give it eternal welfare according to the intention and eternal decree of your infinite wisdom and mercy, I shall enjoy true and secure peace. Now, O Lord, You have prepared and placed before all mortals Your divine light that it may shine upon the world and that all who wish may enjoy it throughout the universe and derive therefrom guidance and salvation. For this is the light which is revealed to the gentiles for the glory of your chosen people of Israel."

10. At the moment when the priest Simeon mentioned the sword and the sign of contradiction, which were prophetical of the passion and death of the Lord, the child bowed its head. Thereby, and by many interior acts of obedience, Jesus ratified the prophecy of the priest and accepted it as the sentence of the Eternal Father pronounced by His minister.

All this the loving mother noticed and understood; she presently began to feel the sorrow predicted by Simeon and thus, in advance, was she wounded by the sword, of which she had been warned. As in a mirror her spirit was made to see all the mysteries included in this prophecy; how her most holy son was to be the stone of stumbling, the perdition of the unbelievers, and the salvation of the faithful; the fall of the synagogue and the establishment of the Church among the heathens; she foresaw the triumph to be gained over the devils and over death, but also that a great price was to be paid for it, namely the frightful agony and death of the cross. She foresaw the boundless opposition and contradiction, which the Lord Jesus was to sustain both personally and in His Church. At the same time she also saw the glory and excellence of the predestined souls. Most holy Mary knew it all and in the joy and sorrow of her most pure soul, excited by the prophecies of Simeon and these hidden mysteries, she performed heroic acts of virtue. All these sayings and happenings were indelibly impressed upon her memory and of all that she understood and experienced. She forgot not the least iota. At all times she looked upon her most holy son with such a living sorrow, as we, mere human creatures with hearts so full of ingratitude, shall never be able to feel. The holy spouse saint Joseph was by these prophecies also made to see many of the mysteries of the Redemption and of the labours and sufferings of Jesus. But the Lord did not reveal them to him so copiously and openly as they were perceived and understood by his heavenly spouse; for in him these revelations were to serve a different purpose, and besides, saint Joseph was not to be an eye-witness of them during his mortal life.

GLORY BE TO THE FATHER   Glory be to the Father, and to the Son, and to the Holy Spirit, as it was in the beginning, is now and ever shall be, world without end. Amen.

THE FATIMA PRAYER   O my Jesus, forgive us our sins, save us from the fires of hell, lead all souls to heaven, especially those in most need of Thy mercy.

The Finding of the Boy Jesus in the Temple

THE FRUIT OF THIS MYSTERY

To seek Christ and never to be satisfied with anything other than Him

BESIDES AVAILING HIMSELF OF the great concourse of people, our Lord was obliged to use also supernatural means to elude the attention of His solicitous mother; for without it she could no more have lost sight of Him than of the sun that lighted her on the way. Therefore, at the parting of the men and the women which I mentioned, the almighty Lord visited His heavenly mother with an abstractive vision of the Divinity, which with divine power centred and withdrew all her faculties toward her interior. She thus remained so abstracted, inflamed and deprived of her senses, that she could make use of them only in so far as was necessary to pursue her way. As to all the rest, she was entirely lost in the sweetness and consolation of the divine vision. Saint Joseph was also wrapped in a most exalted contemplation, which made more easy and mysterious his error in regard to the whereabouts of the child. Thus Jesus withdrew Himself from them, remaining in Jerusalem. When after a considerable while the Queen came to herself and found herself without the company of her most holy son, she supposed Him to be with His reputed father. It was very near to the gate of the city, that the divine child turned and hastened back through the streets. Foreseeing in His divine foreknowledge all that was to happen, He offered it up to His Eternal Father for the benefit of souls. He asked for alms during these three days in order to ennoble from that time on the life of a humble mendicant. He visited the hospitals of the poor, consoling them and giving them the alms which He had received; secretly He restored bodily health to some and spiritual health to many, by enlightening them interiorly and leading them back to the way of salvation. Thus He has fulfilled from that time on the promise, which He was afterwards to make to His Church; that He who gives to the just and to the prophet in the name of a prophet, shall receive the reward of the just.

OUR FATHER   Our Father, Who art in Heaven, hallowed be Thy name, Thy kingdom come, Thy will be done, on earth as it is in heaven. Give us this day our daily bread; and forgive us our trespasses, as we forgive those who trespass against us; and lead us not into temptation, but deliver us from evil. Amen.

HAIL MARY (10)   Hail Mary, Full of Grace, the Lord is with thee. Blessed art thou among women and blessed is the fruit of thy womb, Jesus. Holy Mary, mother of God, pray for us sinners now, and at the hour of our death. Amen.

1. Mary and Joseph repeated their visit to the temple at the feast of the unleavened bread every year. Also when the divine child was twelve years old and when it was time to allow the splendours of His inaccessible and divine light to shine forth, they went to the temple for this feast. This festival of the unleavened bread lasted seven days, according to the command of the divine law; and the more solemn days were the first and the last. Having thus spent all the seven days of the feast they began their journey home to Nazareth. When Our Lord's parents were departing, the child Jesus withdrew from them without their knowledge. For this purpose the Lord availed Himself of the separation of the men and women, which had become customary among the pilgrims for reasons of decency as well as for greater recollection during their return homeward. The children which accompanied their parents were taken in charge either by the men or the women, since their company with either was a matter of indifference. Thus it happened that saint Joseph could easily suppose that the child Jesus

had remained with His most holy mother; with whom He generally remained. The thought that she would go without Him was far from his mind, since the heavenly Queen loved and delighted in Him more than any other creature human or angelic. The great lady did not have so many reasons for supposing that her most holy son was in the company of saint Joseph, but the Lord Himself so diverted her thoughts by holy and divine contemplations, that she did not notice His absence at first. When afterwards she became aware of her not being accompanied by her sweetest and beloved Son, she supposed that the blessed Joseph had taken Him along and that the Lord accompanied His foster father for his consolation.

2. Holy Mary and Joseph pursued their home journey for an entire day. As the pilgrims proceeded onwards they gradually thinned out, each taking his own direction and joining again with his wife or family. The most holy Mary and saint Joseph found themselves at length in the place where they had agreed to meet on the first evening after leaving Jerusalem. When the great lady saw that the child was not with saint Joseph and when the holy Patriarch found that He was not with His mother, the two were struck dumb with amazement and surprise for quite a while. Both, governed in their judgment by their most profound humility, felt overwhelmed with self reproach at their remissness in watching over their most holy son and thus blamed themselves for His absence; for neither of them had any suspicion of the mysterious manner in which He had been able to elude their vigilance. After a time they recovered somewhat from their astonishment and with deepest

sorrow took counsel with each other as to what was to be done. The loving mother said to saint Joseph, "My spouse and my master, my heart cannot rest, unless we return with all haste to Jerusalem in order to seek my most holy son." This they proceeded to do, beginning their search among their relations and friends, of whom, however, none could give them any information or any comfort in their sorrow; on the contrary their answers only increased their anxiety, since none of them had so much as seen their son since their departure from Jerusalem.

3. The afflicted mother turned to her holy angels. These, who numbered ten thousand, she asked, saying, "My friends and companions, you well know the cause of my sorrow, in this bitter affliction be my consolation and give me some information concerning my Beloved, so that I may seek and find Him. Give some relief to my wounded heart, which, torn from its happiness and life, bounds from its place in search of Him." The holy angels, who, though they never lost sight of the Creator and Redeemer, were aware that the Lord wished to furnish His mother this occasion of great merit, and that it was not yet time to reveal the secret to her, answered by speaking to her words of consolation without manifesting to her the whereabouts and the doings of their Lord. This evasive answer raised new doubts in the most prudent lady. Her anxiety of heart caused her to break out in tears and sighs of inmost grief, and urged her onward in search, not of the lost drachma, like the woman in the Gospel, but of the whole treasure of heaven and earth.

4. The mother of wisdom then began to discuss within her heart the different possibilities. The first thought which presented itself to her, was the fear lest Archelaus, imitating the cruelty of his father Herod, should have obtained notice of the presence of Jesus and have taken Him prisoner. Although she knew from the Holy Scriptures and revelations, and by her conversations with her most holy son and teacher, that the time for His passion and death had not yet come and that the king would not take away His life, yet she was filled with dread at the thought, that they should have taken Him prisoner and might ill-treat Him. In her profoundest humility she also had misgivings, lest perchance she had in any way displeased Him by her conduct and therefore deserved that He should leave her and take up His abode in the desert with His precursor saint John.

5. Addressing her absent Love, she exclaimed, "Where shall I go and where shall I find You, Light of my eyes? Do You wish to deprive me of life by the sword of severance from Your presence? Why, O my Lord, have You enriched me with the delights of your infancy, if I am so soon to lose the assistance of Your loving instruction?" Thus this sincerest dove persevered in her tears and groans without cessation or rest, without sleeping or eating anything for three whole days. Although the ten thousand angels accompanied her in corporeal forms and witnessed her affliction and sorrow, yet they gave her no clue to find her lost child. On the third day the great Queen resolved to seek Him in the desert where saint John was; for since she saw no indications that Archelaus had taken Him prisoner, she began to believe more firmly, that her most holy son was with saint John. When

she was about to execute her resolve and was on the point
of departing for the desert, the holy angels detained her,
urging her not to undertake the journey, since the Divine
Word was not there. She wanted also to go to Bethlehem,
in the hope of finding Him in the cave of the Nativity;
but this the holy angels likewise prevented, telling her that
He was not so far off. Although the blessed mother heard
these answers and well perceived that the holy angels knew
the whereabouts of the child Jesus, she was so considerate
and reserved in her humility and prudence, that she gave
no response, nor asked where she could find Him; for she
understood that they withheld this information by command of the Lord. With such magnanimous reverence did
the Queen of the angels treat the wonders of the Most
High and of His ministers and ambassadors. This was one
of the occasions in which the greatness of her queenly and
magnanimous heart was made manifest.

6. With greatest diligence holy Mary sought the child for
three successive days, roaming through the streets of the city,
asking different persons and describing to the daughters of
Jerusalem the marks of her Beloved, searching the byways
and the open squares of the city and thereby fulfilling what
was recorded in the Canticles of Solomon. Some of the
women asked her what were the distinctive marks of her lost
and only son; and she answered all the words of the spouse,
"My Beloved is white and ruddy, chosen out of thousands."
One of the women, hearing her thus describing Him, said,
"This child, with those same marks, came yesterday to my
door to ask for alms, and I gave some to Him; and His
grace and beauty have ravished my heart. And when I gave

Him alms, I felt myself overcome by compassion to see a child so gracious in poverty and want." These were the first news the sorrowful mother heard of her Only Begotten in Jerusalem. A little softened in her sorrow, she pursued her quest and met other persons, who spoke of Him in like manner. Guided by this information she directed her steps to the hospital of the city, thinking that among the afflicted she would find the lover of poverty among His own legitimate brethren and friends. Inquiring at that place, she was informed that a child of that description had paid His visits to the inmates, leaving some alms and speaking words of much consolation to the afflicted. The report of these doings of her Beloved caused sentiments of sweetest and most tender affection in the heart of the heavenly lady, which she sent forth from her inmost heart as messengers to her lost and absent son. Then the thought struck her, that, since He was not with the poor, He no doubt tarried in the temple, as in the house of God and of prayer.

7. The holy angels encouraged her and said, "Our Queen and lady, the hour of your consolation is at hand, soon will you see the Light of your eyes; hasten your footsteps and go to the temple." The glorious patriarch saint Joseph at this moment again met his spouse, for, in order to increase their chance of finding the divine child, they had separated in different directions. By another angel he had now been likewise ordered to proceed to the temple. During all these three days he had suffered unspeakable sorrow and affliction, hastening from one place to another, sometimes without his heavenly spouse, sometimes with her. He was in serious danger of losing his life during this time, if the hand of the

Lord had not strengthened him and if the most prudent lady had not consoled him and forced him to take some food and rest. His sincere and exquisite love for the divine child made him so anxious and solicitous to find Him, that he would have allowed himself no time or care to take nourishment for the support of nature. Following the advice of the holy princes, the most pure Mary and Joseph betook themselves to the temple.

8. Having thus busied Himself with the works of His Father for three days, on the third day the Lord Jesus remained in the temple. The rabbis and the teachers of the temple met in a certain part of the temple in order to confer among themselves concerning some doubtful points of Holy Scriptures. On this occasion the coming of the Messiah was being discussed. The opinions of the scribes were much at variance on this question and the majority held the false opinion that the messiah's immediate coming would be as a victorious king. As the Lord had come into the world in order to give testimony of the truth, which He Himself was, He would not, on this occasion, when it was so important to manifest the truth, allow that error should be confirmed and established by the authority of the learned. The divine child spoke to them as follows, "We must realise that the Messiah is to come twice; once to redeem the world through suffering and a second time to judge it; the prophecies must be applied to both these comings, giving to each one its right explanation."

9. The scribes and learned men who heard Him were all dumbfounded. Convinced by His arguments they looked at

each other and in great astonishment asked, "What miracle is this? And what prodigy of a boy! Who is the child and where has He come from?" But though thus astonished, they did not recognise or suspect who it might be. During this time, and before Jesus had finished His argument, His most holy mother and saint Joseph her most chaste spouse arrived, just in time to hear Him advance His last arguments. When He had finished, all the teachers of the law arose with stupendous amazement. The heavenly lady, absorbed in joy, approached her most loving son and in the presence of the whole assembly said to Him, "Son, why have You done this to us? Behold your father and I have sought You sorrowing". This loving complaint the heavenly mother uttered with equal reverence and affection, adoring Him as God and manifesting her maternal affliction. The Lord answered, "Why is it that you sought Me? Did you not know that I must be about My Father's business?"

10. The Evangelist says that they did not understand the mystery of these words; for it was hidden at the time to most holy Mary and saint Joseph. And for two reasons; on the one hand, the interior joy of now reaping what they had sown in so much sorrow, and the visible presence of their precious treasure, entirely filled the faculties of their souls; and on the other hand, the time for the full comprehension of what had just been treated of in this discussion had not yet arrived for them. The learned men departed, commenting in their amazement upon the wonderful event, by which they had been privileged to hear the teaching of Eternal Wisdom, though they did not recognise it. Being thus left almost alone, the blessed mother, embracing Him

with maternal affection, said to Him, "Permit my longing heart, my son, to give expression to its sorrow and pain; so that it may not die of grief as long as it can be of use to You. Do not cast me off from Your sight; but accept me as Your slave. If it was my negligence, which deprived me of Your presence, pardon me and make me worthy of Your company, and do not punish me with Your absence." The divine child received her with signs of pleasure and offered Himself as her Teacher and Companion until the proper time should arrive. Thus was the dovelike and affectionate heart of the great lady appeased, and they departed for Nazareth.

GLORY BE TO THE FATHER   Glory be to the Father, and to the Son, and to the Holy Spirit, as it was in the beginning, is now and ever shall be, world without end. Amen.

THE FATIMA PRAYER   O my Jesus, forgive us our sins, save us from the fires of hell, lead all souls to heaven, especially those in most need of Thy mercy.

CONCLUDING PRAYERS   *Upon completing the recitation of the Holy Rosary, the following prayers are customary, but others too may be added according to one's devotion and preference.*

HAIL HOLY QUEEN   Hail Holy Queen, mother of Mercy, hail our life, our sweetness and our hope. To thee do we cry, poor banished children of Eve, to thee do we send up our sighs, mourning and weeping in this vale of tears. Turn then, most gracious advocate, thine eyes of mercy towards us, and after this, our exile, show unto us the blessed fruit of thy womb, Jesus. O clement, O loving, O sweet Virgin

Mary. Pray for us O holy mother of God, that we may be made worthy of the promises of Christ.

Let Us Pray   O God, Whose only begotten son, by His life, death and resurrection, has purchased for us the rewards of eternal life, grant we beseech Thee, that meditating on these mysteries of the most Holy Rosary of the Blessed Virgin Mary, we may both imitate what they contain and obtain what they promise, through the same Christ our Lord. Amen.

PRAYER TO SAINT MICHAEL THE ARCHANGEL   Holy Michael, Archangel, defend us in the day of battle. Be our safeguard against the wickedness and snares of the devil. May God rebuke him, we humbly pray; and do thou, O Prince of the heavenly hosts, by the power of God thrust down into hell Satan and all the evil spirits who wander through the world seeking the ruin of souls. Amen.

MEMORARE   Remember, O most gracious Virgin Mary, that never was it known that anyone who fled to thy protection, implored thy help, or sought thine intercession was left unaided. Inspired by this confidence, I fly unto thee, O Virgin of virgins, my mother; to thee do I come, before you I stand, sinful and sorrowful. O mother of the Word Incarnate, despise not my petitions, but in thy mercy hear and answer me. Amen.

May the Divine Assistance remain always with us, and may the souls of the faithful departed, through the mercy of God rest in peace. Amen.

The Sorrowful Mysteries

The Agony in the Garden

THE FRUIT OF THIS MYSTERY

Conformity with the Will of God

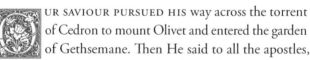

UR SAVIOUR PURSUED HIS way across the torrent of Cedron to mount Olivet and entered the garden of Gethsemane. Then He said to all the apostles, "Wait for Me, and seat yourselves here while I go a short distance from here to pray; you also pray, in order that you may not enter into temptation." The Divine Master gave them this advice, in order that they might be firm in the temptations, of which He had spoken to them at the supper. Then the Master of Life, leaving the band of eight apostles at that place and taking with Him saint Peter, saint John, and saint James, retired to another place, where they could neither be seen nor heard by the rest. Being with the three apostles He raised His eyes up to the Eternal Father confessing and praising Him as was His custom; while interiorly Christ our Lord offered Himself anew to the Eternal Father in satisfaction of His justice for the rescue of the human race; and He gave consent, that all the torments of His passion and death be let loose over that part of His human being which was capable of suffering. From that moment He suspended and restrained whatever consolation or relief would otherwise overflow from the impassible to the passible part of His being, so that in this dereliction His passion and sufferings might reach the highest degree possible. The Eternal Father granted these petitions and approved this total sacrifice of the sacred humanity.

OUR FATHER   Our Father, Who art in Heaven, hallowed be Thy name, Thy kingdom come, Thy will be done, on earth as it is in heaven. Give us this day our daily bread; and forgive us our trespasses, as we forgive those who trespass against us; and lead us not into temptation, but deliver us from evil. Amen.

HAIL MARY (10)   Hail Mary, Full of Grace, the Lord is with thee. Blessed art thou among women and blessed is the fruit of thy womb, Jesus. Holy Mary, mother of God, pray for us sinners now, and at the hour of our death. Amen.

1. The Thursday night of His last supper having already advanced some hours, He chose to go forth to that dreadful battle of His suffering and death by which the Redemption was to be accomplished. The Lord then rose to depart from the hall of the miraculous feast and also most holy Mary left her retreat in order to meet Him on the way. At this face to face meeting of the Prince of eternity and of the Queen, a sword of sorrow pierced the heart of son and mother, inflicting a pang of grief beyond all human and angelic thought. The sorrowful mother threw herself at the feet of Jesus, adoring Him as her true God and Redeemer. The Lord, looking upon her with a majesty divine and at the same time with the overflowing love of a son, spoke to her only these words, "My mother, I shall be with you in tribulation; let us accomplish the will of the Eternal Father and the salvation of men." The great Queen offered herself as a sacrifice with her whole heart and asked His blessing. Having received this she returned to her retirement, where, by a special favour of the Lord, she was enabled to see all that passed in connection with her divine son. Thus she was enabled to accompany Him and cooperate with Him in His activity as far as devolved upon her. The owner of the house, who was present at this meeting, moved by a divine impulse, offered his house and all that it contained to the mistress of heaven, asking her to make use of all that was his during her stay in Jerusalem; and the Queen accepted his offer with humble thanks. The thousand angels of her guard, in forms visible to her, together with some of the pious women of her company, remained with the lady.

2. Judas, alert in his treacherous solicitude for the betrayal of his Divine Master, conjectured that Jesus intended to pass the night in prayer as was His custom. This appeared to him a most opportune occasion for delivering his Master into the hands of his confederates, the scribes and the Pharisees. Having taken this dire resolve, he lagged behind and permitted the Master and his apostles to proceed. Unnoticed by the latter he lost them from view and departed in all haste to his own ruin and destruction. Within him was the turmoil of sudden fear and anxiety, interior witnesses of the wicked deed he was about to commit. Driven on in the stormy hurricane of thoughts raised by his bad conscience, he arrived breathless at the house of the high priests. On the way it happened, that Lucifer, perceiving the haste of Judas in procuring the death of Jesus Christ, and, fearing that after all Jesus might be the true Messiah, came toward him in the shape of a very wicked man, a friend of Judas acquainted with the intended betrayal. In this shape Lucifer could speak to Judas without being recognised. He tried to persuade him that this project of selling his Master did at first seem advisable on account of the wicked deeds attributed to Jesus; but that, having more maturely considered the matter, he did not now deem it advisable to deliver Him over to the priests and Pharisees.; for Jesus was not so bad as Judas might imagine; nor did He deserve death; and besides He might free Himself by some miracles and involve His betrayer into great difficulties. But Judas, filled with fear and an abominable avarice, took no account of the counsel of Lucifer, although he had no suspicion of his not being the friend, whose shape the devil had assumed.

Being stripped of grace Judas neither desired, nor could be persuaded by anyone, to turn back in his malice.

3. Our Redeemer and Master left the house of the Cenacle with all the men who had been present at the celebration of the mysterious supper; and soon many of them dispersed in the different streets in order to attend to their own affairs. Followed by His twelve apostles, the Lord directed His steps toward mount Olivet outside and close to the eastern walls of Jerusalem. The priests, having heard that the Author of Life was in Jerusalem, had gathered to consult about the promised betrayal. Judas entered and told them that he had left his Master with the other disciples on their way to mount Olivet; that this seemed to be the most favourable occasion for His arrest, since on this night they had already made sufficient preparation and taken enough precaution to prevent His escaping their hands by His artifices and cunning tricks. The sacrilegious priests were much rejoiced and began to busy themselves to procure an armed force for the arrest of the most innocent Lamb. All that happened the great lady observed from her retreat. The sorrow which then penetrated the chaste heart of the Virgin Mother, the acts of virtue which she elicited at the sight of such wickedness, and what else she then did, cannot be properly explained by us; we can only say that in all she acted with the plenitude of wisdom and holiness, and with the approbation of the Most Holy Trinity. She pitied Judas and wept over the loss of that perfidious disciple. She sought to make recompense for his malice by adoring, confessing, praising and loving the Lord, whom he delivered by such fiendish and insulting treachery.

4. The Lord began to be sorrowful and feel the anguish of His soul and therefore said to the apostles, "My soul is sorrowful unto death." The Lord permitted this sorrow to reach the highest degree both naturally and miraculously possible in His sacred humanity. This sorrow penetrated not only all the lower faculties of His human life in so far as His natural appetites were concerned; but also all the highest faculties of His body and soul, by which He perceived the inscrutable judgments and decrees of the divine justice, and the reprobation of so many, for whom He was to die. This was indeed by far the greater source of His sorrow. He did not say that He was sorrowful on account of His death, but unto death; for the sorrow naturally arising from the repugnance to the death He was about to undergo, was a minor fear. This interior disturbance and fear confounded and confused the apostles without their daring to speak of it. Moreover, by the sight of His affliction and anxiety they were to take heart at the fears and anxieties of their own souls. The three apostles were exhorted by the Author of Life by the words, "Wait for Me, watch and pray with Me." With this exhortation the Lord separated Himself a short distance from the three apostles. He threw Himself with His divine face upon the ground and prayed to the Eternal Father, "Father, if it is possible, let this chalice pass from Me."

5. I understood therefore that in this prayer Christ besought His Father to let this chalice of dying for the reprobate pass from Him. Whilst dying for His friends and for the predestined was pleasing to the Lord and longingly desired by Him; to die for the reprobate was bitter and painful. Since now His death was not to be evaded, He asked that

none, if possible, should be lost; He pleaded, that as His Redemption would be superabundant for all, that therefore it should be applied to all in such a way as to make all, if possible, profit by it in an efficacious manner; and if this was not possible, He would resign Himself to the will of His Eternal Father. Our Saviour repeated this prayer three times at different intervals, pleading the longer in His agony in view of the importance and immensity of the object in question. According to our way of understanding, there was a contention or altercation between the most sacred humanity and the Divinity of Christ. For this humanity, in its intense love for men who were of His own nature, desired that all should attain eternal salvation through His passion; while His Divinity, in its secret and high judgments, had fixed the number of the predestined and in its divine equity could not concede its blessings to those who so much despised them, and who, of their own free will, made themselves unworthy of eternal life by repelling the kind intentions of Him who procured and offered it to them. From this conflict arose the agony of Christ, in which He prayed so long and in which He appealed so earnestly to the power and majesty of His omnipotent and Eternal Father.

6. This agony of Christ our Saviour grew in proportion to the greatness of His charity and the certainty of His knowledge, that men would persist in neglecting to profit by His passion and death. His agony increased to such an extent, that great drops of bloody sweat were pressed from Him, which flowed to the very earth. Although this prayer was uttered subject to a condition and failed in regard to the reprobate who fell under this condition; yet He gained

thereby a greater abundance and secured a greater frequency of favours for mortals. Through it the blessings were multiplied for those who placed no obstacles, the fruits of the Redemption were applied to the saints and to the just more abundantly, and many gifts and graces, of which the reprobates made themselves unworthy, were diverted to the elect. The human will of Christ, conforming itself to that of the Divinity, then accepted suffering for each respectively, for the reprobate, as sufficient to procure them the necessary help, if they would make use of its merits, and for the predestined, as an efficacious means, of which they would avail themselves to secure their salvation by cooperating with grace. Thus was set in order, and as it were realised, the salvation of the mystical body of His holy Church, of which Christ the Lord was the Creator and Head.

7. As a ratification of this divine decree, while yet our Master was in His agony, the Eternal Father sent the Archangel Michael to the earth in order to comfort Him by a sensible message and confirmation of what He already knew by the infused science of His most holy soul; for the angel could not tell our Lord anything He did not know, nor could he produce any additional effect on His interior consciousness for this purpose. But, as Christ had suspended the consolation, which He could have derived from His human nature from this knowledge and love, leaving it to its full capacity for suffering, He was recompensed to a certain extent, as far as His human senses were concerned, by this embassy of the archangel. He received an experimental knowledge of what He had before known by interior consciousness; that it was not possible for those to be saved who were unwilling; that

the delight of the Eternal Father in the number of the just, although smaller than the number of the reprobate was great; that among the former was His most holy mother, a worthy fruit of His Redemption; that His Redemption would also bear its fruits in the Patriarchs, Prophets, apostles, Martyrs, Virgins and Confessors, who should signalise themselves in His love and perform admirable works for the exaltation of the name of the Most High. Among these the angel moreover mentioned some of the founders of religious orders and the deeds of each one.

8. During the intervals of Christ's prayer He returned to visit the apostles and to exhort them to watch and pray lest they enter into temptation. This the most vigilant Pastor did in order to show the dignitaries of His Church what care and supervision they were to exercise over their flocks. For if Christ, on account of His solicitude for them interrupted His prayer, which was so important, it was in order to teach them, how they must postpone other enterprises and interests to the salvation of their subjects. In order to understand the need of the apostles, I must mention, that the infernal dragon, after having been routed from the Cenacle and forced into the infernal caverns, was permitted by the Saviour again to come forth, in order that he might, by his malicious attempts, help to fulfil the decrees of the Lord. At one fell swoop many of these demons rushed to meet Judas and, in the manner already described, to hinder him, if possible, from consummating the treacherous bargain. As they could not dissuade him, they turned their attention to the other apostles, suspecting that they had received some great favour at the hands of the Lord in the Cenacle.

What this favour was Lucifer sought to find out, in order
to counteract it. Our Saviour saw this cruelty and wrath
of the prince of darkness and his ministers; therefore as a
most loving Father and vigilant Superior He hastened to the
assistance of His little children and newly acquired subjects,
His apostles. He roused them and exhorted them to watch
and pray against their enemies, in order that they might
not enter unawares and unprovided into the threatening
temptation. He spoke to Peter and said to him, "Simon,
are you sleeping? Could you not watch one hour?" And
immediately He added, "Watch and pray that you do not
enter into temptation; for My enemies and your enemies
do not sleep as you do."

9. The Queen of heaven and the holy women of her company had retired to the Cenacle. From her retreat, by divine
enlightenment, she saw most clearly all the mysteries and
doings of her most holy son in the garden. At the moment
when the Saviour separated Himself with the three apostles
Peter, John and James, the heavenly Queen separated herself
from the other women and went into another room. Upon
leaving them she exhorted them to pray and watch lest they
enter into temptation, but she took with her the three Marys,
treating Mary Magdalen as the superior of the rest. Secluding
herself with these three as her more intimate companions,
she begged the Eternal Father to suspend in her all human
alleviation and comfort, both in the sensitive and in the
spiritual part of her being, so that nothing might hinder
her from suffering to the highest degree in union with her
divine son. She prayed that she might be permitted to feel
and participate in her virginal body all the pains of the

wounds and tortures about to be undergone by Jesus. This petition was granted by the Blessed Trinity and the mother in consequence suffered all the torments of her most holy son in exact duplication. She, as far as was possible to her and as far as she knew it to be conformable to the human will of her son, continued her prayers and petitions, feeling the same agony as that of the Saviour in the garden. She also returned at the same intervals to her companions to exhort them, because she knew of the wrath of the demon against them. She was visited by the Archangel Saint Gabriel, as Christ her son was visited by the Archangel Michael. The most prudent lady was provided with some cloths for what was to happen in the passion of her most beloved Son; and on this occasion she sent some of her angels with a towel to the garden in which her son was then perspiring blood, in order to wipe off and dry His venerable countenance. The Lord, for love of His mother and for her greater merit, permitted these ministers of the Most High to fulfil her pious and tender wishes. When the moment for the capture of our Saviour had arrived, it was announced to the three Marys by the sorrowful mother. All three bewailed this indignity with most bitter tears, especially Mary Magdalen, who stood out from the others in the tender love and piety she held for her Master.

10. At the instigation of Judas the Pharisees hastily gathered together a large band of people, composed of pagan soldiers, a tribune and many Jews. Having consigned to them Judas as a hostage, they sent this band on its way to apprehend the most innocent Lamb, who was awaiting them and who was aware of all the thoughts and schemes

of the sacrilegious priests, as foretold expressly by Jeremiah. While they were approaching, the Lord returned the third time to His apostles and, finding them asleep, said to them, "The hour is come; behold the Son of man shall be betrayed into the hands of sinners. Rise up, let us go. Behold he that will betray Me is at hand." The signal of the kiss having been given by Judas, the Lord with His disciples and the soldiers who had come to capture Him came face to face, forming two squadrons, the most opposed and hostile that ever the world saw. Surrounding these wicked soldiers were a multitude of demons, inciting and assisting Judas and his helpers boldly to lay their sacrilegious hands upon their Creator. With unfathomable love for suffering and great force and authority the Lord then spoke to the soldiers, saying, "Whom do you seek?" They answered, "Jesus of Nazareth". Jesus said to them, "I am He". By these inestimably precious and blessed words Christ declared Himself as our Redeemer and Saviour.

GLORY BE TO THE FATHER   Glory be to the Father, and to the Son, and to the Holy Spirit, as it was in the beginning, is now and ever shall be, world without end. Amen.

THE FATIMA PRAYER   O my Jesus, forgive us our sins, save us from the fires of hell, lead all souls to heaven, especially those in most need of Thy mercy.

The Scourging at the Pillar

THE FRUIT OF THIS MYSTERY

A resolution to practice mortification

WO AT A TIME, the Roman soldiers began to scourge Him with such inhuman cruelty, as was possible only in men possessed by Lucifer. The first two scourged the innocent Saviour with hard and thick cords, full of rough knots, and in their sacrilegious fury strained all the powers of their body to inflict the blows. This first scourging raised in the deified body of the Lord deep bruises and livid sores, so that the sacred blood gathered beneath the skin and disfigured His entire body. Already it began to ooze through the wounds. The first two having at length desisted, the second pair continued the scourging, and with hardened leather whips they levelled their strokes upon the places already raw and caused the discoloured sores to break open and shed forth the sacred blood until it bespattered and drenched the garments of the sacrilegious torturers, running down also in streams to the pavement. Those two gave way to the third pair of scourges, who commenced to beat the Lord with barbed sticks. They scourged Him still more cruelly, because they were wounding, not so much His virginal body, as cutting into the wounds already produced by the previous scourging. Besides, they had been secretly incited to greater fury by the demons, who were filled with new rage at the patience of Christ. As the veins of the sacred body had now been opened and His whole Person seemed but one continued wound, the third pair found no more room for new wounds. Their ceaseless blows inhumanly tore the immaculate and virginal flesh of Christ our Redeemer and scattered many pieces of it about the pavement; so much so that a large portion of the shoulder bones were exposed and showed red through the flowing blood; in other places also the bones were laid bare larger than the palm of the hand.

OUR FATHER   Our Father, Who art in Heaven, hallowed be Thy name, Thy kingdom come, Thy will be done, on earth as it is in heaven. Give us this day our daily bread; and forgive us our trespasses, as we forgive those who trespass against us; and lead us not into temptation, but deliver us from evil. Amen.

HAIL MARY (10) Hail Mary, Full of Grace, the Lord is with thee. Blessed art thou among women and blessed is the fruit of thy womb, Jesus. Holy Mary, mother of God, pray for us sinners now, and at the hour of our death. Amen.

1. After our Saviour Jesus was seized by the soldiers His prophecy at the supper was fulfilled. For when the apostles saw their Divine Master taken prisoner and when they perceived that neither His meekness, nor His words, nor His miracles could appease the envy of the priests and Pharisees, they fell into great trouble and affliction. Naturally the fear of personal danger diminished their courage and confidence in the counsels of their Master, and beginning to wander in their faith, each one became possessed with anxious thoughts as to how he could escape the threatening persecutions foreshadowed by what had happened to their Captain and Master. The apostles, availing themselves of the preoccupation of the soldiers and servants in binding and fettering the meek Lamb of God, betook themselves to flight unnoticed. Certainly their enemies, if they had been permitted by the Author of Life, would have captured all the apostles, especially if they had seen them fly like cowards or criminals. But it was not proper that they should be taken and made to suffer at that time. This was clearly indicated as the will of the Lord, when He said, that if they sought Him, they should let His companions go free; these words had the force of a divine decree and were verified in the event. For the hatred of the priests and Pharisees extended to the apostles, and was deep enough to make them desire the death of all of them. They separated from each other,

with only saint Peter and saint John keeping each other company to follow their God and Master from a distance.

2. Having been taken prisoner and firmly bound, the most meek Lamb Jesus was dragged from the garden to the house of the high priests, first to the house of Annas. The turbulent band of soldiers and servants, having been advised by the traitorous disciple that His Master was a sorcerer and could easily escape their hands, if they did not carefully bind and chain Him securely before starting on their way, took all precautions inspired by such a mistrust. Lucifer and his compeers of darkness secretly irritated and provoked them to increase their impious and sacrilegious ill-treatment of the Lord beyond any bounds of humanity and decency. As they were willing accomplices of Lucifer's malice, they omitted no outrage against the person of their Creator within the limits set them by the Almighty. Many times they violently threw Him to the ground and as His hands were tied behind He fell upon it with His divine countenance and was severely wounded and lacerated. In His falls they pounced upon Him, inflicting blows and kicks trampling upon His body and upon His head and face. After Jesus had been thus insulted and struck in the house of Annas, He was sent, bound and fettered as He was, to the priest Caiaphas, the son in-law of Annas, who in that year officiated as the prince and high priest; with him were gathered the scribes and distinguished men of the Jews in order to urge the condemnation of the most innocent Lamb.

3. The high priest Caiaphas, filled with a deadly envy and hatred against the Master of Life, was seated in his chair of

state or throne. With him were Lucifer and all his demons, who had come from the house of Annas. The scribes and Pharisees, like bloodthirsty wolves, surrounded the gentle Lamb; all of them were full of the exultation of the envious, who see the object of their envy confounded and brought down. By common consent they sought for witnesses, whom they could bribe to bring false testimonies against Jesus our Saviour. Those that had been procured, advanced to proffer their accusations and testimony; but their accusations neither agreed with each other, nor could any of their slander be made to apply to Him, who of His very nature was innocence and holiness. Lucifer, who incited the high priest and all the rest, intently watched the conduct of the Saviour. But the intention of the dragon was different from that of the high priest. He merely wanted to irritate the Lord, or to hear some word, by which he could ascertain whether He was true God. With this purpose Satan stirred up Caiaphas to the highest pitch of rage and to ask in great wrath and haughtiness, "I adjure You by the living God, that You tell us, if You are the Christ, the Son of God." Out of reverence for the name of God Our Lord Jesus answered, "I am He". All exclaimed in a loud voice, "He is guilty of death, let Him die, let Him die!" Roused by Satanic fury they all fell upon their most meek Master and discharged upon Him their wrath. Lucifer and his devils could not bear Our Lord's divine response and the utterance of the Holy Name; they immediately felt a superior force, which hurled them down into the abyss and oppressed them by the truth He had uttered.

4. The order of the council of wickedness was executed; the servants dragged the Creator of heaven and earth to that polluted and subterranean dungeon there to imprison Him. The Saviour was alone in the dungeon, surrounded by the angelic spirits, who were full of admiration at the doings and the secret judgments of the Lord in what He wished to suffer. They adored Him with deepest reverence and magnified His holy name in exalted praise. The Redeemer of the world addressed a long prayer to His Eternal Father for the children of the Catholic Church, for the spreading of the holy faith, and for the apostles, especially for saint Peter, who during that time was weeping his sin. He prayed also for those who had injured and tormented Him; above all He included in His prayer His most holy mother and all those who in imitation of Him were to be afflicted and despised in this world. At the same time He offered up His passion and His coming death for these ends. His grief-stricken mother followed Him in these prayers, offering up the same petitions for the children of the Church and for its enemies without any movements of anger, indignation or dislike toward them. Only against the demon was she incensed, because he was entirely incapable of grace on account of his irreparable obstinacy. At the dawn of Friday morning the executioners brought our Saviour Jesus Christ to the house of Pilate, in order to present Him, still bound with the same chains and ropes in which they had taken Him from the garden, before his tribunal.

5. In their wrath the Jews were anxious to dispose Pilate favourably toward their project and they wished him to pronounce the sentence of death against Jesus without the least

delay. When they perceived his hesitation, they ferociously raised their voices, accusing Jesus over and over again of revolting against the government of Judea, deceiving and stirring up the people, calling Himself Christ, that is an anointed King. Pilate could see that they were so determined on the death of Jesus that it would be difficult to satisfy them without consenting to their demands; but at the same time he clearly saw that they persecuted Him out of mortal envy and that their accusations about His disturbing the people, were false and ridiculous. He impiously considered that a severe scourging of the innocent Jesus would placate the fury of the ungrateful people and soothe the envy of the priests and the scribes. But Pilate was entirely wrong in his judgment and acted like an ignorant man. Placed between the known truth and worldly considerations, Pilate chose to follow the erroneous leading of the latter, and he ordered Jesus to be severely scourged, though he had himself declared Him as free from guilt.

6. Thereupon the ministers of Satan brought Jesus our Saviour to the place of punishment, which was a courtyard or enclosure attached to the house and set apart for the torture of criminals in order to force them to confess their crimes. It was enclosed by a low, open building, surrounded by columns, some of which supported the roof, while others were lower and stood free. To one of these columns, which was of marble, they bound Jesus very securely; for they still thought Him a magician and feared His escape. In loosening the ropes and chains, which He had borne since His capture in the garden, they cruelly widened the wounds which His bonds had made in His arms and wrists. Having freed His

hands, they commanded Him with infamous blasphemies to despoil Himself of the seamless tunic which He wore. The Son of the Eternal Father obeyed the executioners and began to unclothe Himself, ready to bear the shame of the exposure of His most sacred and modest body before such a multitude of people. With the exception of a strip of cloth for a cincture, which He wore beneath the tunic and with which His mother likewise had clothed Him in Egypt, the Lord stood now naked. These garments had grown with His sacred body, and the Almighty did not will for them to be removed. All the six of His tormentors separately made an attempt to remove them with the same result., they were hindered and physically paralysed. This miraculous occurrence did not, however, move or soften the hearts of these human beasts; but in their diabolical insanity they attributed it all to the supposed sorcery and witchcraft of the Author of Truth and Life.

7. The cruel scourging was not solely aimed at our Lord's back, but also His face, hands and feet. The blows to these parts were unspeakably painful, given the presence of many sensitive and delicate nerves. His venerable countenance became so swollen and wounded that the blood and the swellings blinded Him. In addition to their blows the executioners spat upon Him and blasphemed Him. The exact number of blows dealt out to the Saviour from head to foot was 5,115. The great Lord and Author of all creation who, by His divine nature was incapable of suffering, was, in His human flesh and for our sake, reduced to a man of sorrows as prophesied, and was made to experience our infirmities, becoming the last of men, a man of sorrows

and the outcast of the people. In order to wipe out entirely that beauty, which exceeded that of all other men, they beat Him to excess, thus leaving unwounded not a single spot in which they could exert their fury and wrath against the most innocent Lamb. The divine blood flowed to the ground, gathering here and there in great abundance.

8. The multitudes who had followed the Lord filled up the courtyard of Pilate's house and the surrounding streets; for all of them waited for the issue of this event, discussing and arguing about it according to each one's views. Amid all this confusion the Virgin Mother endured unheard of insults, and she was deeply afflicted by the injuries and blasphemies heaped upon her divine son by the Jews and gentiles. When they brought Jesus to the scourging place she retired in the company of the Marys and saint John to a corner of the courtyard. Assisted by her divine visions, she there witnessed all the scourging and the torments of our Saviour. Although she did not see it with the eyes of her body nothing was hidden to her, no more than if she had been standing quite near. Human thoughts cannot comprehend how great and how diverse were the afflictions and sorrows of the great Queen and mistress of the angels, together with many other mysteries of the Divinity they shall become manifest in the next life, for the glory of the son and mother. Although she shed no blood except what flowed from her eyes with her tears, nor was she lacerated in her flesh; yet the bodily pains so changed and disfigured her, that saint John and the holy women failed to find in her any resemblance of herself. Besides the tortures of the body she suffered ineffable sorrows of the soul; there sorrow was

augmented in proportion to the immensity of her insight. For her sorrows flowed not only from the natural love of a mother and a supreme love of Christ as her God, but it was proportioned to her power of judging more accurately than all creatures of the innocence of Christ, the dignity of His divine Person, the atrocity of the insults coming from the perfidious Jews and the children of Adam, whom He was freeing from eternal death.

9. Having at length executed the sentence of scourging, the executioners unbound the Lord from the column, and with imperious and blasphemous presumption commanded Him immediately to put on His garment. But while they had scourged the most meek Master, one of His tormentors, instigated by the devil, had hidden His clothes out of sight, in order to prolong the nakedness and exposure of His divine Person for their derision and sport. This evil purpose suggested by the devil, was well known to the mother of the Lord. She therefore, making use of her power as Queen, commanded Lucifer and all his demons to leave the neighbourhood, and immediately, compelled by her sovereign power and virtue, they fled. She gave orders that the tunic be brought by the holy angels within reach of her most holy son, so that He could again cover His sacred and lacerated body. All this was immediately attended to, although the sacrilegious executioners understood not the miracle, nor how it had come to pass; they attributed it all to the sorcery and magic of the demon. During this protracted nakedness our Saviour had, in addition to His wounds, suffered from the cold of exposure. His sacred blood had frozen and compressed the wounds, which had become inflamed and

extremely painful; the cold had diminished His powers of resistance, although the fire of His infinite charity strained them to the utmost in order to suffer more and more.

10. The sins and depraved lives of the Christians proclaim louder than tongues their abuse of the blood of Christ and their consent to the guilt in His death which they load upon themselves. They seem to cry out, "Let Christ be affronted, spat upon, buffeted, stretched upon a cross, despised, let Him yield to Barabbas and die; let Him be tormented, scourged and crowned with thorns for our sins, let His blood interest us no more than that it flow copiously and be imputed to us for all eternity, let the incarnate God suffer and die; if only we are left free to enjoy the apparent goods of this world, to seize the pleasing hour, to use creatures for our comfort, to hoard up riches, engage in all deceits, forgive no injuries, entertain the delights of carnal pleasures, let our eyes see nothing that they shall not covet. Let us have all this and let Christ be crucified." Ask the damned in hell, whether these were not their sentiments in this life, they will be forced to admit that it was so. What else except damnation can they expect, who abuse the blood of Christ and waste it upon themselves. Though this divine Blood was intended to wash and cleanse all the children of Adam, and though it was in effect poured out upon all the children of the holy Church, yet there are many belonging to it who make themselves guilty of this blood by their works in the same manner as the Jews of old charged themselves with it, both by word and deed.

GLORY BE TO THE FATHER   Glory be to the Father, and
to the Son, and to the Holy Spirit, as it was in the beginning,
is now and ever shall be, world without end. Amen.

THE FATIMA PRAYER   O my Jesus, forgive us our sins,
save us from the fires of hell, lead all souls to heaven, especially those in most need of Thy mercy.

The Crowning with Thorns

THE FRUIT OF THIS MYSTERY

Sorrow for failing to display my faith outwardly

HE BLESSED VIRGIN SAID to the saint, "If you see your Redeemer, your spouse and your Lord tormented, afflicted, crowned with thorns and saturated with reproaches and at the same time desires to have a part in Him and be a member of His mystical body, it is not becoming, or even possible, that you live steeped in the pleasures of the flesh. The Almighty would indeed have been powerful enough to exalt His predestined in this world, to give them riches and favours beyond those of others, to make them strong as lions for reducing the rest of mankind to their invincible power. But it was inopportune to exalt them in this manner, in order that men might not be led into the error of thinking that greatness consists in what is visible and happiness in earthly goods; lest, being induced to forsake virtues and obscure the glory of the Lord, they fail to experience the efficacy of divine grace and cease to aspire toward spiritual and eternal things. This is the science which I wish you to study continually and in which you must advance day by day, putting into practice all that you learn to understand and know."

OUR FATHER   Our Father, Who art in Heaven, hallowed be Thy name, Thy kingdom come, Thy will be done, on earth as it is in heaven. Give us this day our daily bread; and forgive us our trespasses, as we forgive those who trespass against us; and lead us not into temptation, but deliver us from evil. Amen.

HAIL MARY (10)   Hail Mary, Full of Grace, the Lord is with thee. Blessed art thou among women and blessed is the fruit of thy womb, Jesus. Holy Mary, mother of God, pray for us sinners now, and at the hour of our death. Amen.

1. Thereupon they took Jesus to the praetorium, where, with the same cruelty and contempt, they again despoiled Him of His garments and in order to deride Him before all the people as a counterfeit king, clothed Him in a much torn and soiled mantle of purple colour. They placed also upon His sacred head a cap made of woven thorns, to serve Him

as a crown. This cap was woven of thorn branches and in such a manner that many of the hard and sharp thorns would penetrate into the skull, some of them to the ears and others to the eyes. Hence one of the greatest tortures suffered by the Lord was that of the crown of thorns.

2. Instead of a sceptre they placed into His hands a contemptible reed. They also threw over His shoulders a violet coloured mantle, something of the style of copes worn in churches; for such a garment belonged to the vestiture of a king. In this array of a mock king the perfidious Jews decked Him out, who by His nature and by every right was the King of Kings and the Lord of Lords. Then all the soldiers, in the presence of the priests and Pharisees, gathered around Him and heaped upon Him their blasphemous mockery and derision. Some of them bent their knees and mockingly said to Him, "God save You, King of the Jews". Others buffeted Him; others snatched the cane from His hands and struck Him on His crowned head; others spat upon Him; all of them, instigated by furious demons, insulted and affronted Him in different ways.

3. O charity incomprehensible and exceeding all measure! O patience never seen or imagined among mortals! Who, O my Lord and God, since You are the true and mighty God both in essence and in Your works, who could oblige You to suffer the humiliation of such unheard of torments, insults and blasphemies? On the contrary, O my God, who among men has not done many things which offend You and which should have caused You to refuse suffering and to deny them your favour? Who could ever believe all this,

if we knew not of Your infinite goodness. But now, since we see it and in firm faith look upon such admirable blessings and miracles of love, where is our judgment? What effect upon us has the light of truth? What enchantment is this that we suffer, since at the very sight of Your sorrows, scourges, thorns, insults and affronts, we seek for ourselves, without the least shame or fear, the delights, the riches, the ease, the preferments and vanities of this world? Truly, great is the number of fools, since the greatest foolishness and dishonesty is to recognise a debt and be unwilling to pay it; to receive blessings and never give thanks for them; to have before one's eyes the greater good, and despise it; to claim it for ourselves and make no use of it; to turn away and fly from life, and seek eternal death.

4. It seemed to Pilate that the spectacle of a man so ill-treated as Jesus of Nazareth would move and fill with shame the hearts of that ungrateful people. He therefore commanded Jesus to be brought from the praetorium to an open window, where all could see Him crowned with thorns, disfigured by the scourging and the ignominious vestiture of a mock king. Pilate himself spoke to the people, calling out to them, "Behold the man!", as if he had said, "See this Man, whom you hold as your enemy! What more can I do with Him than to have punished Him in this severe manner? You certainly have nothing more to fear from Him. I do not find any cause of death in Him." What this judge said was certainly the full truth; but in his own words he committed an outrageous injustice, since, knowing and confessing that this Man was just and not guilty of death, he had nevertheless ordered Him to be tormented and punished in such a way

that, according to the natural course, He should have been killed many times over. O blindness of self love! O hellish malice of estimating only the influence of those who can confer or take away mere earthly dignities, rather than the judgment of Him, who rewards or condemns for all eternity.

5. In the house of Pilate, through the ministry of the holy angels, our Queen was placed in such a position that she could hear the disputes of the iniquitous judge with the scribes and priests concerning the innocence of Christ our Saviour, and concerning the release of Barabbas in preference to Him. All the clamours of these human tigers she heard in silence and admirable meekness, as the living counterpart of her most holy son. Although she preserved the unchanging propriety and modesty of her exterior, all the malicious words of the Jews pierced her sorrowful heart like a two-edged sword. But the voices of her unspoken sorrows resounded in the ears of the Eternal Father more pleasantly and sweetly than the lamentation of the beautiful Rachel who, as Jeremiah says, was weeping her children because they were no more. Our most beautiful Rachel, the purest Mary, sought not revenge, but pardon for her enemies, who were depriving her of the Only Begotten of the Father and her only son. She imitated all the actions of the most holy soul of Christ and accompanied Him in the works of most exalted holiness and perfection; for neither could her torments hinder her charity, nor her affliction diminish her fervour, nor could the tumult distract her attention, nor the outrageous injuries of the multitudes prevent her interior recollection, under all circumstances she practised the most exalted virtues in the most eminent degree.

6. When the Blessed among women, most holy Mary, saw her divine son as Pilate showed Him to the people and heard him say, "Ecce homo!", she fell upon her knees and openly adored Him as the true God-Man. The same was also done by saint John and the holy women, together with all the holy angels of the Queen and lady; for they saw that not only Mary, as the Mother of the Saviour, but that God Himself desired them to do so. The most prudent lady spoke to the Eternal Father, to the angels and especially to her most beloved Son precious words of sorrow, compassion and profound reverence, possible to be conceived only in her chaste and loving heart.

7. While Pilate was thus disputing with the Jews in the praetorium, his wife, Procula, happened to hear of his doings and she sent him a message telling him, "What have you to do with this Man? Let Him go free; for I warn you that I have had this very day some visions in regard to Him!" This warning of Procula originated through the activity of Lucifer and his demons. For they, observing all that was happening in regard to the person of Christ and the unchangeable patience with which He bore all injuries, were more and more confused and staggered in their rabid fury. Although the swollen pride of Lucifer could not explain how His Divinity could ever subject Itself to such great insults, nor how He could permit His body to suffer such ill-treatment, and although he could not come to any certain conviction, whether this Jesus was a God-Man or not; yet the dragon was persuaded, that some great mystery was here transpiring among men which would be the cause of great damage and defeat to him and his malice if he did not succeed in

arresting its progress in the world. Having come to this conclusion with his demons, he many times suggested to the Pharisees the propriety of ceasing their persecutions of Christ. These suggestions, however, since they originated from malice and were void of any power for good, failed to move the obstinate and perverted hearts of the Jews. Despairing of success the demons betook themselves to the wife of Pilate and spoke to her in dreams, representing to her that this Man was just and without guilt, that if her husband should sentence Him he would be deprived of his rank and she herself would meet with great adversity. They urged her to advise Pilate to release Jesus and punish Barabbas, if she did not wish to draw misfortune upon their house and their persons.

8. But the Jews, on the contrary, demanded that Christ be crucified. Thereupon Pilate asked for water and released Barabbas. Then he washed his hands in the presence of all the people, saying, "I have no share in the death of this just Man, whom you condemn. I wash my hands in order that you may understand they are not sullied in the blood of the Innocent." Pilate foolishly thought that by this ceremony he could excuse himself entirely and that he thereby could put its blame upon the princes of the Jews and upon the people who demanded it. The wrath of the Jews was so blind and foolish that for the satisfaction of seeing Jesus crucified, they entered upon this agreement with Pilate and took upon themselves and upon their children the responsibility for this crime. Loudly proclaiming this terrible sentence and curse, they exclaimed, "His blood come upon us and upon our children". O most foolish and cruel blindness!

O inconceivable rashness! The unjust condemnation of the Just and the blood of the Innocent, whom the judge himself is forced to proclaim guiltless, do you wish to take upon yourselves and upon your children, in order that His blood may call out against you to the end of the world?

9. Pilate withdrew with Jesus into the praetorium, where, speaking with Him alone, he asked where He was from. The Lord did not answer this question; for Pilate was not in a state of mind either to understand or to merit a reply. Nevertheless he insisted and said to the King of Heaven, "Do You then not speak to me? Do You not know, that I have power to crucify You and power to dismiss You?" Pilate sought to move Him to defend Himself and tell him what he wanted to know. It seemed to Pilate that a man so wretched and tormented would gladly accept any offer of favour from a judge. But the Master of Truth answered Pilate without defending Himself but with unexpected dignity; for He said, "You should not have any power against Me, unless it were given you from above. Therefore, he that has delivered Me to you, has the greater sin." This answer by itself made the condemnation of Christ inexcusable in Pilate; since he could have understood therefore, that neither he nor Caesar had any power of jurisdiction over this man Jesus; that by a much higher decree He had been so unreasonably and unjustly delivered over to his judgment; that therefore Judas and the priests had committed a greater sin than he in not releasing Him; and that nevertheless he too was guilty of the same crime, though not in such high degree. Pilate failed to arrive at these mysterious truths; but he was struck with still greater consternation at the words of Christ our

Lord, and therefore made still more strenuous efforts to liberate Him. The priests, who were now abundantly aware of his intentions, threatened him with the displeasure of the emperor, which he would incur, if he permitted this One, who had aspired to be king, to escape death. Pilate was much disturbed at the malicious and threatening intimation of the Jews, and seating himself in his tribunal at the sixth hour in order to pass sentence upon the Lord, he once more turned to plead with the Jews, saying, "Behold your King!" And all of them answered, "Away with Him, away with Him, crucify Him!" He replied, "Shall I crucify your King?" Whereupon they shouted unanimously, "We have no king but Caesar."

10. Pilate permitted himself to be overcome by the obstinacy and malice of the Jews. On the day of Passover then, seated in his tribunal, he pronounced the sentence of death against the Author of Life. The Jews departed from the hall in great exultation and joy, proclaiming the sentence of the most innocent Lamb. All this was well known to the sorrowful mother, who, though outside of the hall of judgment, saw all the proceedings by exalted vision. When the priests and Pharisees rushed forth exulting in the condemnation of Christ to the death of the cross, the pure heart of this most blessed mother was filled with new sorrow and was pierced and transfixed with the sword of unalleviated bitterness. Since the sorrow of most holy Mary on this occasion surpassed all that can enter the thoughts of man, it is useless to speak more of it, and it must be referred to the pious meditation of Christians.

GLORY BE TO THE FATHER   Glory be to the Father, and to the Son, and to the Holy Spirit, as it was in the beginning, is now and ever shall be, world without end. Amen.

THE FATIMA PRAYER   O my Jesus, forgive us our sins, save us from the fires of hell, lead all souls to heaven, especially those in most need of Thy mercy.

The Carrying of the Cross

THE FRUIT OF THIS MYSTERY
The decision to carry the cross with Our Lord

S OUR LORD CARRIED the heavy cross, His executioners, bare of all human compassion and kindness, dragged Him along with incredible cruelty and insults. Some of them jerked Him forward by the ropes in order to accelerate His passage, while others pulled from behind in order to hinder it. On account of this jerking and the weight of the cross they caused Him to sway to and fro and often to fall to the ground. By the hard knocks

He thus received on the rough stones great wounds were opened, especially on the two knees and they were widened at each repeated fall. The heavy cross also inflicted a wound on the shoulder on which it was carried. The unsteadiness caused the cross sometimes to knock against His sacred head, and sometimes the head against the cross; thus the thorns of His crown penetrated deeper and wounded the parts which they had not yet reached. To these torments of the body the ministers of evil added many insulting words and affronts, spitting on Him and throwing the dirt of the pavement into His face so mercilessly, that they blinded the eyes that looked upon them with such divine mercy. Thus they of their own account condemned themselves to the loss of the graces, with which His very looks were fraught. By the haste with which they dragged Him along in their eagerness to see Him die, they did not allow Him to catch His breath; for His most innocent body, having been in so few hours overwhelmed with such a storm of torments, was so weakened and bruised, that to all appearances He was ready to yield up life under His pains and sorrows.

OUR FATHER   Our Father, Who art in Heaven, hallowed be Thy name, Thy kingdom come, Thy will be done, on earth as it is in heaven. Give us this day our daily bread; and forgive us our trespasses, as we forgive those who trespass against us; and lead us not into temptation, but deliver us from evil. Amen.

HAIL MARY (10)   Hail Mary, Full of Grace, the Lord is with thee. Blessed art thou among women and blessed is

the fruit of thy womb, Jesus. Holy Mary, mother of God, pray for us sinners now, and at the hour of our death. Amen.

1. To the great satisfaction and joy of the priests and Pharisees, Pilate then decreed the sentence of death on the cross against Life itself, Jesus our Saviour and He was dressed, once again, in His own clothes. The Jews wished to see Him undergo the punishment of the cross in His own clothes so that in them He might be recognised by all. Only by His garments could He now be recognised by the people, since His face had been disfigured beyond recognition by the scourging, the impure spittle, and the crown of thorns. They again clothed Him with the seamless tunic, which at the command of the Queen was brought to Him by the angels; for the executioners had thrown it into a corner of another room in the house, where they left it to place upon Him the mocking and scandalous purple cloak. But the Jews neither understood nor noticed any of these circumstances, since they were too much taken up with the desire of hastening His death.

2. Through the diligence of the Jews in spreading the news of the sentence decreed against Jesus of Nazareth, the people hastened in multitudes to the house of Pilate in order to see Him brought forth to execution. Since the ordinary number of inhabitants was increased by the gathering of numerous strangers from different parts to celebrate the Pasch, the city was full of people. All of them were stirred by the news and filled the streets up to the very palace of Pilate. It was a Friday, the day of preparation for the ensuing Sabbath, their greatest feast, on which no servile work was to

be performed, not even such as cooking meals. In the sight of all these multitudes they brought forth our Saviour. At the sight of such a sorrowful spectacle a confused shouting and clamour arose from the people, so that nothing could be understood, but all formed one uproar and confusion of voices. But above all the rest were heard the shouts of the priests and Pharisees, who in their unrestrained joy and exultation harangued the people to become quiet and clear the streets through which the divine Victim was to pass, in order that they might hear the sentence of death proclaimed against Him. The people were divided and confused in their opinions, according to the suggestions of their own hearts. At this spectacle a number of people were present who had benefited from the miracles and the kindness of Jesus, and some of them had become His followers and friends. These now showed their sympathy, some in bitter tears, others by asking what this Man had done to deserve such punishment; others were dumbfounded and began to be troubled and distressed by this confusion and uproar.

3. The sentence of Pilate against our Saviour having been published in a loud voice before all the people, the executioners loaded the heavy cross, on which He was to be crucified, upon His tender and wounded shoulders. In order that He might carry it they loosened the bonds holding His hands, but not the others, since they wished to drag Him along by the loose ends of the ropes that bound His body. In order to torment Him the more they drew two loops around His throat. The cross was fifteen feet long, of thick and heavy timbers. The herald began to proclaim the sentence and the whole confused and turbulent multitude of the people,

the executioners and soldiers, with great noise, uproar and disorder began to move from the house of Pilate to mount Calvary through the streets of Jerusalem. The Master and Redeemer of the world, Jesus, before receiving the cross, looked upon it with a countenance full of extreme joy and exultation such as would be shown by a bridegroom looking at the rich adornments of His bride, and on receiving it, He addressed it as follows, "O cross, beloved of My soul, now prepared and ready to still My longings, come to Me, that I may be received in your arms, and that, attached to them as on an altar, I may be accepted by the Eternal Father as the sacrifice of His everlasting reconciliation with the human race."

4. None of these sacred mysteries and happenings were hidden from the great lady of the world, Mary; for she had a most intimate knowledge and understanding of them, far beyond that of all the angels. The events, which she could not see with the eyes of her body, she perceived by her intelligence and revealed science, which manifested to her the interior operation of her most holy son. By this divine light she recognised the infinite value of the wood of the cross after once it had come in contact with the deified humanity of Jesus our Redeemer. Immediately she venerated and adored it in a manner befitting it. The same was also done by the heavenly spirits attending upon the Queen. She imitated her divine son in the tokens of affections, with which He received the cross, addressing it in the words suited to her office as Coadjutrix of the Redeemer. By her prayers to the Eternal Father she followed Him in His exalted sentiments as the living original and exemplar, without failing in the least

point. When she heard the voice of the herald publishing and rehearsing the sentence through the streets, the heavenly mother, in protest against the accusations contained in the sentence and in the form of comments on the glory and honour of the Lord, composed a canticle of praise and worship of the innocence and sinlessness of her all holy son and God. In the composing of this canticle the holy angels helped her, conjointly with them she arranged and repeated it, while the inhabitants of Jerusalem were blaspheming their own Creator and Saviour.

5. Our Saviour proceeded on the way to Calvary bearing upon His shoulders, according to the saying of Isaiah, His own government and principality, which was none else than His cross, from whence He was to subject and govern the world, meriting thereby that His name should be exalted above all other names and rescuing the human race from the tyrannical power of the demon over the sons of Adam. In order to destroy this tyrant and break the sceptre of his reign and the yoke of our servitude, Christ our Saviour placed the cross upon His shoulders; namely, upon that place, where are borne both the yoke of slavery and the sceptre of royal power. He wished to intimate thereby, that He despoiled the demon of this power and transferred it to His own shoulders, in order that thenceforward the captive children of Adam should recognise Him for their legitimate Lord and true King. All mortals were to follow Him in the way of the cross and learn, that by this cross they were subjected to His power and now become His vassals and servants, bought by His own lifeblood.

6. Beyond all human thought and estimation was the sorrow of the most sincere dove and Virgin Mother while she thus witnessed with her own eyes her son carrying the cross to Mount Calvary; for she alone could fittingly know and love Him according to His true worth. It would have been impossible for her to live through this ordeal, if the divine power had not strengthened her and preserved her life. With bitterest sorrow she addressed the Lord and spoke to Him in her heart, "My son and Eternal God, light of my eyes and life of my soul, receive, O Lord, the sacrifice of my not being able to relieve You of the burden of the cross and carry it myself, who am a daughter of Adam; for it is I who should die upon it in love of You, as You now wish to die in most ardent love of the human race. O most loving Mediator between guilt and justice! How do You cherish mercy in the midst of so great injuries and such heinous offences? O charity without measure or bounds! O infinite and sweetest love, would that the hearts and the wills of men were all mine, so that they could give heartfelt thanks for all that You endure! O who will speak to the hearts of the mortals to teach them what they owe to You, since You have paid so dearly for their salvation from ruin!"

7. The sorrowful and stricken mother followed with the multitudes on the way of her divine son, accompanied by saint John and the pious women. As the surging crowds hindered her from getting very near to the Lord, she asked the Eternal Father to be permitted to stand at the foot of the cross of her blessed son and see Him die with her own eyes. With the divine consent she ordered her holy angels to manage things in such a way as to make it possible for

her to execute her wishes. The holy angels obeyed her with great reverence; and they speedily led the Queen through some by-street, in order that she might meet her son. Thus it came that both of them met face to face in sweetest recognition of each other and in mutual renewal of each other's interior sorrows. Yet they did not speak to one another, nor would the fierce cruelty of the executioners have permitted such an encounter. But the most prudent mother adored her divine son and true God, laden with the cross; and interiorly besought Him, that, since she could not relieve Him of the weight of the cross and since she was not permitted to command her holy angels to lighten it, He would inspire these ministers of cruelty to procure some one for His assistance. This prayer was heard by the Lord Christ; and so it happened, that Simon of Cyrene was afterwards impressed to carry the cross with the Lord. The Pharisees and the executioners were moved to this measure, some of them out of natural compassion, others for fear lest Christ, the Author of Life, should lose His life by exhaustion before it could be taken from Him on the cross.

8. In fulfilment of the prayerful wish of the blessed mother, the Pharisees and ministers were inspired with the resolve to engage someone to help Jesus our Saviour in carrying the cross to mount Calvary. At this juncture, Simon, of Cyrene, the father of the disciples Alexander and Rufus, happened to come along. He was called by this name because he was a native of Cyrene, a city of Libya, and had come to Jerusalem. This Simon was now forced by the Jews to carry the cross a part of the way. They themselves would not touch it, indeed, they would not even come near it, as being the instrument

of punishment for One whom they held to be a notorious malefactor. By this pretended caution and avoidance of His cross they sought to impress the people with a horror for Jesus. The Cyrenean took hold of the cross and Jesus was made to follow between the two thieves, in order that all might believe Him to be a criminal and malefactor like to them. The Virgin Mother walked very closely behind Jesus, as she had desired and asked from the Eternal Father. To His divine will she so conformed herself in all the labours and torments of her son that, witnessing with her own eyes and partaking of all the sufferings of her son in her blessed soul and in her body, she never allowed any sentiment or wish to arise interiorly or exteriorly, which could be interpreted as regret for the sacrifice she had made in offering her son for the death of the cross and its sufferings. Her charity and love of men, and her grace and holiness, were so great, that she vanquished all these movements of her human nature.

9. Our Saviour then, the new and true Isaac, the Son of the Eternal Father, reached the mountain of sacrifice, which is the same one to which His prototype and figure, Isaac, was brought by the patriarch Abraham. Upon the most innocent Lamb of God was to be executed the rigour of the sentence, which had been suspended in favour of the son of the Patriarch. Mount Calvary was held to be a place of defilement and ignominy, as being reserved for the chastisement of condemned criminals, whose corpses spread around it their stench and attached to it a still more evil fame. Our most loving Jesus arrived at its summit so worn out, wounded, torn and disfigured, that He seemed altogether transformed into an object of pain and sorrows. The power

of the Divinity, which deified His most holy humanity by its hypostatical union, helped Him, not to lighten His pains, but to strengthen Him against death; so that, still retaining life until death should be permitted to take it away on the cross, He might satiate His love to the fullest extent. The sorrowful and afflicted mother, in the bitterness of her soul, also arrived at the summit of the mount and remained very close to her divine son; but in the sorrows of her soul she was as it were beside herself, being entirety transformed by her love and by the pains which she saw Jesus suffer. Near her were saint John and the three Marys; for they alone, through her intercession and the favour of the Eternal Father, had obtained the privilege of remaining so constantly near to the Saviour and to His cross.

10. It was already the sixth hour, which corresponds to our noontime, and the executioners, intending to crucify the Saviour naked, despoiled Him of the seamless tunic and of His garments. As the tunic was large and without opening in front, they pulled it over the head of Jesus without taking off the crown of thorns; but on account of the rudeness with which they proceeded, they inhumanly tore off the crown with the tunic. Thus they opened anew all the wounds of His head, and in some of them remained the thorns, which, in spite of their being so hard and sharp, were wrenched off by the violence with which the executioners despoiled Him of His tunic and, with it, of the crown. With heartless cruelty they again forced it down upon His sacred head, opening up wounds upon wounds. By the rude tearing off of the tunic were renewed also the wounds of His whole body, since the tunic had dried into the open places and

its removal added new pains to His wounds. To all these sufferings was added the confusion of being bereft of His garments in the presence of His most blessed mother, of her pious companions, and in full sight of the multitudes gathered around. By His divine power He, however, reserved for Himself the lower garment which His mother had wound around His waist in Egypt; for neither at the scourging, nor at the crucifixion could the executioners remove it, and He was laid in the sepulchre still covered with this cloth. The holy cross was now lying on the ground and the executioners began making the necessary preparations for crucifying Him and, with Him, the two thieves.

GLORY BE TO THE FATHER   Glory be to the Father, and to the Son, and to the Holy Spirit, as it was in the beginning, is now and ever shall be, world without end. Amen.

THE FATIMA PRAYER   O my Jesus, forgive us our sins, save us from the fires of hell, lead all souls to heaven, especially those in most need of Thy mercy.

The Crucifixion of Our Lord

THE FRUIT OF THIS MYSTERY

To take Mary to my home each day, to see her as my mother

AVING FINISHED AND ESTABLISHED the work of Redemption in all its perfection, it was becoming that the Incarnate Word, just as He came forth from the Father to enter mortal life, should enter into immortal life of the Father through death. Therefore Christ our Saviour added the last words uttered by Him, "Father, into Your hands I commend My spirit." The Lord spoke these words in a loud and strong voice, so that the bystanders heard them. In pronouncing them He raised His eyes to heaven, as one speaking with the Eternal Father, and with the last accent He gave up His spirit and inclined His head. By the divine force of these words Lucifer with all his demons were hurled into the deepest caverns of hell, there they lay motionless. The mighty Queen and mother concurred with the will of her son Jesus and In virtue of these decrees of the supreme King and of the Queen, the evil spirits were routed from Calvary and precipitated to deepest hell more violently and suddenly than a flash of light through the riven clouds.

OUR FATHER   Our Father, Who art in Heaven, hallowed be Thy name, Thy kingdom come, Thy will be done, on earth as it is in heaven. Give us this day our daily bread; and forgive us our trespasses, as we forgive those who trespass against us; and lead us not into temptation, but deliver us from evil. Amen.

HAIL MARY (10)   Hail Mary, Full of Grace, the Lord is with thee. Blessed art thou among women and blessed is the fruit of thy womb, Jesus. Holy Mary, mother of God, pray for us sinners now, and at the hour of our death. Amen.

1. In order to make holes for the nails to hammered into, the executioners haughtily commanded the Creator of the universe to stretch Himself out upon the cross. The Teacher of Humility obeyed without hesitation. But they, following their inhuman instinct of cruelty, marked the places for the holes, not according to the size of His body, but larger, having in mind a new torture for their Victim. This inhuman

intent was known to the mother of light, and the knowledge of it was one of the greatest afflictions of her chastest heart during the whole passion. She could not do anything to prevent it, as it was the will of the Lord to suffer these pains for men. When He rose from the cross, and they set about boring the holes, the great lady approached and took hold of one of His hands, adoring Him and kissing it with greatest reverence. The executioners allowed this because they thought that the sight of His mother would cause so much the greater affliction to the Lord; for they wished to spare Him no sorrow they could cause Him. But they were ignorant of the hidden mysteries; for the Lord during His passion had no greater source of consolation and interior joy than to see in the soul of His most blessed mother, the beautiful likeness of Himself and the full fruits of His passion and death. This joy, to a certain extent, comforted Christ our Lord also in that hour.

2. Presently one of the executioners seized the hand of Jesus our Saviour and placed it upon the auger hole, while another hammered a large and rough nail through the palm. The veins and sinews were torn, and the bones of the sacred hand, which made the heavens and all that exists, were forced apart. When they stretched out the other hand, they found that it did not reach up to the auger hole; for the sinews of the other arm had been shortened and the executioners had maliciously set the holes too far apart. In order to overcome the difficulty, they took the chain, with which the Saviour had been bound in the garden, and looping one end through a ring around His wrist, they, with unheard of cruelty, pulled the hand over the hole and fastened it with

another nail. Thereupon they seized His feet, and placing them one above the other, they tied the same chain around both and stretched them with barbarous ferocity down to the third hole. Then they drove through both feet a large nail into the cross. Thus the sacred body, in which dwelled the Divinity, was nailed motionless to the holy cross, the bones of His body, dislocated and forced from their natural position, could all be counted. The bones of His breast, of His shoulders and arms, and of His whole body yielded to the cruel violence and were torn from their sinews.

3. After the Saviour was nailed to the cross, the executioners judged it necessary to bend the points of the nails which projected through the back of the wood, in order that they might not be loosened and drawn out by the weight of the body. For this purpose they raised up the cross in order to turn it over, so that the body of the Lord would rest face downward upon the ground with the weight of the cross upon Him. This new cruelty appalled all the bystanders and a shout of pity arose in the crowd. But the sorrowful and compassionate mother intervened by her prayers, and asked the Eternal Father not to permit this boundless outrage to happen in the way the executioners had intended. She commanded her holy angels to come to the assistance of their Creator. When, therefore, the executioners raised up the cross to let it fall, with the crucified Lord face downward upon the ground, the holy angels supported Him and the cross above the stony and fetid ground, so that His divine countenance did not come in contact with the rocks and pebbles. Thus altogether ignorant of the miracle the executioners bent over the points of the nails; for the sacred

body was so near to the ground and the cross was so firmly held by the angels, that the Jews thought it rested upon the hard rock. Then they dragged the lower end of the cross with the crucified God near to the hole, wherein it was to be planted. Some of them getting under the upper part of the cross with their shoulders, others pushing upward with their lances, they raised the Saviour on His cross and fastened its foot in the hole they had drilled into the ground. Thus our true life and salvation now hung in the air upon the sacred wood in full view of the innumerable multitudes of different nations and countries.

4. When the great Queen of the angels, most holy Mary, perceived that the Jews in their perfidy and envy vied in dishonouring Him, she besought the Eternal Father to see to the honour of His Only Begotten. And so, with the zeal and authority of the Queen of the universe, she addressed all the irrational creatures and said, "Insensible creatures, created by the hand of the Almighty, manifest your compassion, which in deadly foolishness is denied to Him by men capable of reason. O you heavens, you sun, moon and O you stars and planets, stop in your course and suspend your activity in regard to mortals. O you elements, change your condition, earth lose your stability, let your rocks and cliffs be rent. O you sepulchres and monuments of the dead, open and send forth your contents for the confusion of the living. You mystical and figurative veil of the temple, divide into two parts and by your separation threaten the unbelievers with chastisement, give witness to the truth and to the glory of their Creator and Redeemer, which they are trying to obscure." All the inanimate creatures, by divine

will, obeyed the command of the most holy Mary. From the noon hour until three o'clock in the afternoon, which was called the ninth hour, when the Lord expired, they exhibited the great disturbances and changes mentioned in the Gospels. The sun hid its light, the planets showed great alterations, the earth quaked, many mountains were rent; the rocks shook one against the other, the graves opened and sent forth some of the dead alive. The changes in the elements and in the whole universe were so notable and extraordinary that they were evident on the whole earth. All the Jews of Jerusalem were dismayed and astonished; although their outrageous perfidy and malice made them unworthy of the truth and hindered them from accepting what all the insensible creatures preached to them.

5. As the wood of the cross was the throne of His majesty and as He was now raised upon it, Christ now uttered those words of highest charity and perfection, "Father, forgive them, for they do not know what they are doing!" This principle of charity and fraternal love the Divine Teacher had appropriated to Himself and proclaimed by His own lips. He now confirmed and executed it upon the cross, not only pardoning and loving His enemies, but excusing those under the plea of ignorance whose malice had reached the highest point possible to men in persecuting, blaspheming and crucifying their God and Redeemer. Such was the difference between the behaviour of ungrateful men favoured with so great enlightenment, instruction and blessing; and the behaviour of Jesus in His most burning charity while suffering the crown of thorns, the nails, and the cross and unheard of blasphemy at the hands of men.

O incomprehensible love! O ineffable sweetness! a patience inconceivable to man, admirable to the angels and fearful to the devils! One of the two thieves, called Dismas, became aware of some of the mysteries. Being assisted at the same time by the prayers and intercession of most holy Mary, he was interiorly enlightened concerning his Rescuer and Master by the first word on the cross. Moved by true sorrow and contrition for his sins, he turned to Jesus, and said, "Lord, remember me when You shall come into Your kingdom!" In this happiest of thieves, in the centurion, and in the others who confessed Jesus Christ on the cross, began to appear the results of the Redemption. But the one most favoured was this Dismas, who merited to hear the second word of the Saviour on the cross, "Amen, I say to you, this day shall you be with Me in Paradise."

6. Having thus justified the good thief, Jesus turned His loving gaze upon His afflicted mother, who with saint John was standing at the foot of the cross. Speaking to both, He first addressed His mother, saying, "Woman, behold your son!", and then to the apostle, "Behold your mother!" The Lord called her woman and not mother, because this name of mother had in it something of sweetness and consolation, the very pronouncing of which would have been a sensible relief. During His passion He would admit of no exterior consolation, having renounced for that time all exterior alleviation and easement. Moreover, by this word "woman" He tacitly and by implication wished to say, "Blessed among all women". The remaining words to His mother signified, "I am going to My Father and cannot accompany you further; My beloved disciple will attend upon you and serve you as

his mother, and he will be your son." All this the heavenly Queen understood. The holy apostle on his part received her as his own from that hour on; for he was enlightened anew in order to understand and appreciate the greatest treasure of the Divinity in the whole creation next to the humanity of Christ our Saviour. In this light he reverenced and served her for the rest of her life.

7. Christ our Saviour, as the triumphant conqueror, having vanquished the great enemy, now yielded up His spirit to the Father and permitted death to approach by inclining His head. By this permission He also vanquished death, for death could not attack men, nor had any jurisdiction over them, except through the first sin, of which it was a punishment. As our Saviour paid the debt of sin, when death took away His life without the shadow of justice, it lost the power which it had over the other sons of Adam. Thenceforward neither death nor the devil could attack men, unless they, failing to avail themselves of the victory of Christ, should again subject themselves of their own free will. Our Saviour Christ despoiled the demon of all these advantages and, in dying without sin and satisfying for us, merited that our death should be a death of the body only, and not of the soul; that it should have power to take away our temporal life, but not our eternal; the natural, not the spiritual; and that it should thenceforward be merely the portal to the eternal happiness, if we ourselves do not renounce that blessing.

8. The piercing of the Our Lord's side, which could not be felt by the sacred and dead body of the Lord, was felt by the

most blessed mother in His stead, and in the same manner as if her most chaste body had been pierced. But even this pain was exceeded by the affliction of her most holy soul, in witnessing the cruel laceration of her son. At the same time, moved by compassion and love and in forgetfulness of her own sorrow, she said to Longinus, "May the Almighty look upon you with eyes of mercy for the pain you have caused to my soul!" So far and no farther went her indignation. Let her example of meekness ever be of instruction to us all, whenever we are unjustly injured. The retribution sought by Our Lady for the evil-doer was one of great blessing, namely, that God should look upon him with eyes of mercy and return grace on behalf of the offence. Thus it happened that some of the blood and water from His sacred side dropped upon the face of Longinus, not only restoring to him the gift of perfect eyesight, but, even more, perfect light to his soul, enabling him to recognise in the Crucified his Saviour, whom he had so inhumanly mutilated. Through this enlightenment Longinus was converted; weeping over his sins and having washed them in the blood and water of the side of Christ, he openly acknowledged and confessed Him as the true God and Saviour of the world. He proclaimed Him as such in the presence of the Jews, confounding by his testimony their perfidy and hardness of heart.

9. The most prudent Queen then perceived the mystery of the pouring forth of the blood and water: that from His sacred side, as from the roots, should now spread out through the whole world the fruits of life eternal. She conferred within herself also upon the mystery of that rock struck by the rod of divine justice, in order that the living

waters might issue forth, quenching the thirst of all the human race and recreating and refreshing all who betook themselves to drink there from. She considered the coincidence of the five fountains from the wounds of His hands, feet and sides, which opened up the new paradise of the most holy humanity of our Saviour, and which were more copious and powerful to fertilise the earth than those of the terrestrial paradise divided into four streams over the surface of the globe. These and other mysteries the great lady rehearsed in a canticle of praise, which she composed in honour of her divine son after His being wounded by the lance.

10. Some time passed during which the sorrowful mother held at her breast the dead Jesus, and as evening was far advancing, saint John and Joseph of Arimathea besought her to allow the burial of her son to proceed. The most prudent mother yielded; and they now embalmed the sacred body, using all the hundred pounds of the spices and the aromatic ointments brought by Nicodemus. Thus anointed, the deified body was placed on a bier in order to be carried to the sepulchre. The heavenly Queen, most attentive in her zealous love, called from heaven many choirs of angels, who, together with those of her guard, should accompany the burial of their Creator. Immediately they descended from on high in shapes visible to their Queen and lady, though not to the rest. A procession of heavenly spirits was formed and another of men, and the sacred body was borne along by saint John, Joseph, Nicodemus and the centurion, who had confessed the Lord and now assisted at His burial. They were followed by the blessed mother, by Mary Magdalen and

the rest of the women disciples. They proceeded toward a nearby garden, where Joseph had hewn into the rock a new grave, in which nobody had as yet been buried or deposited. In this most blessed sepulchre they placed the sacred body of Jesus. Before they closed it up with the heavy stone, the devout and prudent mother adored Christ anew, causing the admiration of men and angels. They imitated her, all of them adoring the crucified Saviour now resting in His grave; thereupon they closed the sepulchre with the stone, which, according to the Evangelist, was very heavy.

GLORY BE TO THE FATHER   Glory be to the Father, and to the Son, and to the Holy Spirit, as it was in the beginning, is now and ever shall be, world without end. Amen.

THE FATIMA PRAYER   O my Jesus, forgive us our sins, save us from the fires of hell, lead all souls to heaven, especially those in most need of Thy mercy.

CONCLUDING PRAYERS   *Upon completing the recitation of the Holy Rosary, the following prayers are customary, but others too may be added according to one's devotion and preference.*

HAIL HOLY QUEEN   Hail Holy Queen, mother of Mercy, hail our life, our sweetness and our hope. To thee do we cry, poor banished children of Eve, to thee do we send up our sighs, mourning and weeping in this vale of tears. Turn then, most gracious advocate, thine eyes of mercy towards us, and after this, our exile, show unto us the blessed fruit of thy womb, Jesus. O clement, O loving, O sweet Virgin

Mary. Pray for us O holy mother of God, that we may be made worthy of the promises of Christ.

Let Us Pray   O God, Whose only begotten son, by His life, death and resurrection, has purchased for us the rewards of eternal life, grant we beseech Thee, that meditating on these mysteries of the most Holy Rosary of the Blessed Virgin Mary, we may both imitate what they contain and obtain what they promise, through the same Christ our Lord. Amen.

PRAYER TO SAINT MICHAEL THE ARCHANGEL   Holy Michael, Archangel, defend us in the day of battle. Be our safeguard against the wickedness and snares of the devil. May God rebuke him, we humbly pray; and do thou, O Prince of the heavenly hosts, by the power of God thrust down into hell Satan and all the evil spirits who wander through the world seeking the ruin of souls. Amen.

MEMORARE   Remember, O most gracious Virgin Mary, that never was it known that anyone who fled to thy protection, implored thy help, or sought thine intercession was left unaided. Inspired by this confidence, I fly unto thee, O Virgin of virgins, my mother; to thee do I come, before you I stand, sinful and sorrowful. O mother of the Word Incarnate, despise not my petitions, but in thy mercy hear and answer me. Amen.

May the Divine Assistance remain always with us, and may the souls of the faithful departed, through the mercy of God rest in peace. Amen.

The Glorious Mysteries

The Resurrection

FTER JESUS OUR SAVIOUR, arisen and glorified, had visited and filled with glory His most blessed mother, He resolved, as the loving Father and Pastor, to gather the sheep of His flock, which the scandal of His sufferings had disturbed and scattered. The holy Patriarchs and all whom He had rescued from Limbo continually remained in His company, although they did not manifest themselves and remained invisible during His apparitions; only our great Queen was privileged to see them, know them and speak to them all during the time intervening between the Resurrection and the Ascension of her divine son. Whenever the Lord did not appear to others, He remained with His beloved mother in the Cenacle; nor did she ever leave this place during all the forty days. There she enjoyed the presence of the Redeemer of the world and of the choir of Prophets and Saints, by whom the King and Queen were attended. For the purpose of making His Resurrection known to His apostles, He began by showing Himself to the women, not on account of their weakness, but because they were stronger in their belief and in their hope of the Resurrection; for this is the reason why they merited the privilege of being the first to see Him arisen.

OUR FATHER   Our Father, Who art in Heaven, hallowed be Thy name, Thy kingdom come, Thy will be done, on earth as it is in heaven. Give us this day our daily bread; and forgive us our trespasses, as we forgive those who trespass against us; and lead us not into temptation, but deliver us from evil. Amen.

HAIL MARY (10)   Hail Mary, Full of Grace, the Lord is with thee. Blessed art thou among women and blessed is the fruit of thy womb, Jesus. Holy Mary, mother of God, pray for us sinners now, and at the hour of our death. Amen.

1. To the cavern of Limbo the most holy soul of Christ our Lord betook itself in the company of innumerable angels, who gave glory to their victorious and triumphant King. In accordance with His greatness and majesty they commanded

the portals of this ancient prison to be opened, in order that the King of Glory, powerful in battles and Lord of virtues, might find them unlocked and open at His entrance. By the presence of the most holy soul this obscure cavern was converted into a heaven and was filled with a wonderful splendour; and to the souls therein contained was imparted the clear vision of the Divinity. In one instant they passed from the state of long deferred hope to the possession of glory, and from darkness to the inaccessible light, which they now began to enjoy. All of them recognised their true God and Redeemer, and gave Him thanks and glory, breaking forth in canticles of praise. At that moment our first parents, Adam and Eve, saw the havoc wrought by their disobedience, the priceless remedy it necessitated and the immense goodness and mercy of the Redeemer. They then felt the effects of His copious Redemption in the glory of their souls, and praised anew the Omnipotent and Saint of saints, who had with such marvellous wisdom achieved such a salvation. Then the Lord commanded the angels to bring to His presence all the souls in Purgatory, and this was immediately done. They were absolved then and there by the Redeemer from the punishments still due to them, and they were glorified with the other souls of the just by the beatific vision. Thus on that day, through presence of the King, the prison houses of both Limbo and Purgatory were depopulated.

2. The divine soul of Christ our Redeemer remained in Limbo from half past three on Friday until after three of the Sunday morning. During this hour He returned to the sepulchre where many angels had remained, guarding and

venerating the sacred body united to the Divinity. Some
of them, obeying the command of their Queen and mistress, had gathered the relics of the sacred blood shed by
her divine son, the particles of flesh scattered about, the
hair torn from His divine face and head, and all else that
belonged to the perfection and integrity of His most sacred
humanity. On these the mother of prudence lavished her
solicitous care. The angels took charge of these relics, each
one filled with joy at being privileged to hold the particles,
which he was able to secure. Then, in the presence of all holy
patriarch saints, who had came with Him to the sepulchre,
all the relics were reunited to the sacred body, restoring it
to its natural perfection and integrity. This happened in
the same moment that the most holy soul reunited with
the body, giving it immortal life and glory. Instead of the
winding sheets and the ointments, in which it had been
buried, it was clothed with the four gifts of glory, namely,
with clearness, impassibility, agility and subtlety. These gifts
overflowed from the immense glory of the soul of Christ
into the sacred body.

3. Of all these mysteries the great Queen of heaven was
aware and she participated in them from her retreat in the
Cenacle. In the same instant in which the most holy soul
of Christ entered and gave life to His body the joy of her
immaculate soul overflowed into her immaculate body.
The blessed Mary being thus prepared, Christ our Saviour,
arisen and glorious, in the company of all the Saints and
Patriarchs, made His appearance. The ever humble Queen
prostrated herself upon the ground and adored her divine
son; and the Lord raised her up and drew her to Himself. In

this contact, which was more intimate than the contact with the humanity and the wounds of the Saviour sought by Magdalen, the Virgin Mother participated in an extraordinary favour, which she alone, as exempt from sin, could merit. In the midst of this embrace she heard a voice saying to her, "My beloved, ascend higher!" By the power of these words she was entirely transformed and saw the Divinity clearly and intuitively, wherein she found complete, though only temporary, rest and reward for all her sorrows and labours. Silence alone here is proper, since reason and language are entirely inadequate to comprehend or express what passed in the blessed Mary during this beatific vision, the highest she had enjoyed till then.

4. On the Sunday morning, entirely ignorant of the grave's having been sealed and placed under guard by order of Pilate, the holy women arose before dawn in order to execute their pious design of anointing the body of the Lord anew. On their way they thought only of the difficulty of removing the large stone, which they now remembered had been rolled before the opening of the sepulchre; but their love made light of this hindrance, though they did not know how to remove it. When they came forth from the house of the Cenacle, it was yet dark, but before they arrived at the sepulchre the sun had already dawned and risen. The sepulchre was in an arched vault, as in a cave, the entrance to which was covered by a large stone slab. Within, somewhat to one side and raised from the ground, was the hollow slab wherein the body of the Saviour had rested.

5. A little before the women thought and spoke of the difficulty of removing the stone, a violent and wonderful quaking or trembling of the earth took place; at the same time an angel of the Lord opened the sepulchre and cast aside the stone that covered and obstructed the entrance. At this noise and the earthquake the guards of the sepulchre fell prostrate to the earth, struck motionless with fear and consternation, although they did not see the Lord. For the body of the Lord was no more in the grave; He had already arisen and issued from the monument before the angel cast aside the stone. The women, though in some fear, took heart and were encouraged by God to approach and enter the vault. Near the entrance they saw the angel who had thrown aside the stone, seated upon it, refulgent in countenance and in snow white garments. He spoke to them saying, "Be not afraid; you seek Jesus of Nazareth, who was crucified, He is risen, He is not here; behold the place where they laid Him." The holy women entered, and seeing the sepulchre vacant they were filled with grief; for as yet they were more deeply affected at seeing the Lord absent, than by the words of the angel. Then they saw two other angels seated at each end of the slab, who said to them, "Why do you seek the Living among the dead? Remember how He told you He was to rise on the third day. Go, tell His disciples and Peter that He goes before you into Galilee, there you shall see Him."

6. Although the disciples and apostles considered the tale of the women mere preposterous talk, saint Peter and saint John, desirous of convincing themselves with their own eyes, departed in all haste to the sepulchre. Saint John arrived

first, and without entering saw the winding sheets laid to one side. He waited for the arrival of saint Peter, who, passing the other apostle, entered first. Both of them saw that the sacred body was not in the tomb. Saint John was then assured of what he had secretly begun to believe, and openly professed his belief. The two apostles returned to give an account of the wonder they had seen in the sepulchre. The women remained in a place apart from the sepulchre and wonderingly commented on the events. Mary Magdalen, in great excitement and tears, re-entered the sepulchre to look again. Although the apostles had not seen the angels, she saw them and they asked her, "Woman, why are you weeping?" She answered, "Because they have taken away my Lord; and I know not where they have laid Him." With this answer she left the garden where the sepulchre was, and met the Lord. She did not know Him, but thought it was the gardener. And the Lord also asked her, "Woman, why are you weeping? Who are you looking for" Magdalen, ignorant of His being the Lord, answered Him as if He were the gardener and, without further reflection, said, "Sir, if you have taken Him from here, tell me where you have laid Him, and I will take Him away." Then the loving Master said "Mary," and in pronouncing her name He permitted Himself to be recognised by the tone of His voice. As soon as Magdalen recognised Jesus she was aflame with joyous love and answered saying, "Master!" Throwing herself at His feet, she was about to touch and kiss them, as being used to that favour. But the Lord prevented her and said, "Do not touch Me, for I am not yet ascended to My Father from Whom I came; but return and tell my brethren, the

apostles, that I am going to My Father and theirs." Then
Magdalen left, filled with consolation and joy.

7. Shortly after, when Thomas had left the Cenacle and the
doors had been locked, the Lord entered and appeared to
them. In their midst He saluted them, saying, "Peace be with
you. It is I; do not be afraid." At this sudden apparition, the
apostles feared lest what they saw was a ghost or phantasm,
and the Lord added, "Why are you troubled, and why do
such thoughts arise in your hearts? See My hands and feet,
that it is I Myself; handle and see, for a spirit has no flesh
and bones, as you see I have." The apostles were so excited
and confused, that though they saw Him and touched the
wounded hands of the Saviour, they could not realise that
it was He to whom they spoke and whom they touched.
The loving Master in order to assure them still more, said
to them, "Give Me something to eat, if you have anything."
Joyfully they offered Him some fried fish and a honeycomb.
He ate part of these, and divided the rest among them, saying, "Did you not know that all that happened to Me is that
which has been written by the Prophets and that all must
necessarily be fulfilled in Me as it was prophesied?" And at
these words He opened their minds, and they knew Him,
and understood the sayings of the Scriptures concerning His
passion, death and Resurrection on the third day. Having
thus instructed them, He said again, "Peace be with you. As
the Father has sent me, so I send you, in order that you may
teach the world the knowledge of the truth, of God and of
eternal life, preaching repentance for sins and forgiveness
of them in my name." Breathing upon them, He added and
said, "Receive the Holy Spirit, in order that the sins which

you forgive may be forgiven, and those which you do not forgive, may not be forgiven." The Saviour, having thus consoled and confirmed them in faith, and having given them and all priests the power to forgive sins, disappeared from among them.

8. The apostles, after the events in Jerusalem, betook themselves to Galilee; for the Lord had so commanded them and had promised, that they should there see Him. Saint Peter, happening to be with the seven apostles and disciples on the shores of that sea, proposed that they pass the time in fishing, as that was his trade. All of them accompanied him and they spent the night in casting out their nets; but they caught not a single fish. In the morning our Saviour Jesus appeared on the bank without making Himself known. He was near the boat on which they were fishing and He asked them, "Have you something to eat?" They answered, "We have nothing." The Lord replied, "Throw out your net on the right side, and you shall make a catch." They complied and their net became so filled, that they could not lift it into the boat. This miracle caused saint John to recognise the Lord Christ, and going nearer to saint Peter, he said, "It is the Lord who speaks to us from the bank." Then saint Peter likewise recognised Jesus; and immediately seized with his accustomed fervour, he hastily girded himself with the tunic, and cast himself into the sea, walking on the waters to the Master of Life, while the others followed in their boat. They sprang ashore and found that the Lord had already prepared for them a meal; for they saw a fire and upon its glimmering ashes bread and a fish. The Lord however told them to bring some of those they had caught. The Lord

commanded them to eat. Although He was so familiar and affable in His behaviour to them, no one ventured to ask who He was; for the miracles and the majesty of the Lord filled them with great reverence. He divided among them the fish and the bread. As soon as they had finished eating, He turned to saint Peter and said to Him, "Simon, son of John, do you love Me more than these do?" Saint Peter answered, "Yes, Lord, You know that I love You." The Lord replied, "Feed my lambs." Immediately He asked again, "Simon, son of John, do you love me?" Saint Peter gave the same answer, "Lord, You know that I love You." And the Lord put the same question the third time, "Simon, son of John, do you love Me?" At this third repetition Peter grieved and answered, "Lord, You knowe all things, and also that I love You." Christ our Saviour then answered the third time, "Feed my sheep." By these words He made Peter the sole head of His only and universal Church, giving him the supreme vicarious authority over all men. On this account He had questioned him so thoroughly concerning his love, as if that alone could make him capable of the supreme dignity, and of itself sufficed for its worthy exercise.

9. During the forty days after the Resurrection, the Lord remained in the Cenacle and in the company of His most holy mother whenever He was not absent in appearing to some of His chosen friends. All the rest of the time He spent in her presence. Anyone can prudently conjecture, that all this time, in which these two Sovereigns of the world were together, they spent in works altogether divine and above all the conceptions of the human mind. What has been made known to me of these works is ineffable; for

often they would engage in sweetest colloquy of inscrutable wisdom and this conversation was for the loving mother a joy, which though inferior to the beatific vision, was consoling and delightful beyond all that is imaginable. At other times the great Queen, the Patriarchs and Saints, who there assisted in their glorified state, occupied themselves in the praise and exaltation of the Most High. Mary had a deep knowledge of all the works and merits of the saints; of the blessings, favours and gifts each one had received from the Omnipotent; of the mysteries, figures and prophecies which had gone before in the ancient Patriarchs. All this she was mistress of, and it was present to her mind in contemplation more completely, than the Hail Mary is known to us for recitation. The exalted lady considered all the great motives of these saints for praising and blessing the Author of all good. Though they, enjoying the beatific vision, fulfilled and are fulfilling this duty without cessation, yet in their conversations and interactions with the heavenly princess, they were constantly urged by her to magnify and praise the divine Majesty for all these blessings and operations so evident to the eyes of her soul.

10. Our Lady during the greater part of the forty days composed more canticles and hymns than all the saints and Prophets have left for our use. Admirable was also the delight she drew from her conversation with her own holy mother, her father Joachim, saint Joseph, saint John the Baptist, and the great Patriarchs who Our glorified Lord permitted to appear to her during these days. In mortal flesh no state can be imagined, which approaches so close to the beatific fruition as the one enjoyed at that time by the great lady

and Queen. Another wonder happened during those days, which was, that all the souls of the just who died in grace within those forty days, gathered in the Cenacle, and those who had no debt to pay, were there beatified. But those who were subject to Purgatory were obliged to wait in the same place without seeing the Lord, some three, some five days, others again for a shorter or longer period. For the mother of mercy satisfied for their defects by genuflections, penances or some other work of loving piety, through which she applied to them the infinite merits of her divine son. Thus she helped to abbreviate their punishment and the pain of not seeing the Lord and soon they were beatified and admitted to the choir of the saints. For each one that thus joined their ranks, the great lady composed new hymns of praise to the Lord. Amidst all these delights and jubilations the kindest mother, with ineffable generosity, did not forget the misery and poverty of the children of Eve deprived of this glory; but like a true mother of mercy, turning her eyes upon the condition of mortals, she offered for all of them her most fervent prayers. She besought the Eternal Father for the spreading of the Gospel through the world; the multiplication of the children of the Church; for its defence and protection and for the extension of the fruits of the Redemption to all men.

GLORY BE TO THE FATHER   Glory be to the Father, and to the Son, and to the Holy Spirit, as it was in the beginning, is now and ever shall be, world without end. Amen.

THE FATIMA PRAYER   O my Jesus, forgive us our sins, save us from the fires of hell, lead all souls to heaven, especially those in most need of Thy mercy.

The Ascension

THE FRUIT OF THIS MYSTERY

Desire for Heaven

HE MOST AUSPICIOUS HOUR had arrived, in which the Only Begotten of the Eternal Father, after descending from heaven in order to assume human flesh, was to ascend by His own power and in a most wonderful manner to the right hand of God, one and equal with Him in nature and infinite glory. He was to ascend, also, because He had previously descended to the lowest regions of the earth. By this Ascension He sealed all the mysteries and hastened the fulfilment of His promise, according to which He was, with the Father, to send the Paraclete upon His Church after He Himself had ascended into heaven. In order to celebrate this festive and mysterious day, Christ our Lord selected as witnesses the hundred and twenty persons, to whom He had spoken in the Cenacle. They were the most holy Mary, the eleven apostles, the seventy-two disciples, Mary Magdalen, Lazarus their brother, the other Marys and a few other faithful men and women.

OUR FATHER   Our Father, Who art in Heaven, hallowed be Thy name, Thy kingdom come, Thy will be done, on earth as it is in heaven. Give us this day our daily bread; and forgive us our trespasses, as we forgive those who trespass against us; and lead us not into temptation, but deliver us from evil. Amen.

HAIL MARY (10)   Hail Mary, Full of Grace, the Lord is with thee. Blessed art thou among women and blessed is the fruit of thy womb, Jesus. Holy Mary, mother of God, pray for us sinners now, and at the hour of our death. Amen.

1. While the Lord was at table with the eleven apostles, the other disciples and the pious women, He said to them, "My sweetest children, I am about to ascend to My Father, from Whom I descended in order to rescue and save men. I leave with you in My stead My own mother as your Protectress, Consoler and Advocate, and as your mother, whom you are to hear and obey in all things. Just as I have told you, that he who sees Me sees My Father, and he who knows

Me, knows also Him; so I now tell you, that he who knows my mother, knows Me; he who hears her, hears Me; and who honours her, honours Me. All of you shall have her as your mother, as your superior and head, and so shall also your successors. She shall answer your doubts, solve your difficulties; in her, those who seek Me shall always find Me; for I shall remain in her until the end of the world, and I am in her now, although you do not understand how." This the Lord said, because He was sacramentally present in the bosom of His mother; for the sacred species, which she had received at the last supper, were preserved in her until consecration of the first Mass.

2. The Lord added and said, "You will have Peter as the supreme head of the Church, for I leave him as My Vicar; and you shall obey him as the chief high priest. Saint John you shall hold as the son of My mother; for I chose and appointed him for this office on the cross." The Lord then looked upon His most beloved mother, who was there present, and intimated His desire of expressly commanding that whole congregation to love and reverence her in a manner suited to the dignity of Mother of God, and of leaving this command under form of a precept for the whole Church. But the most humble lady besought her Only Begotten to be pleased not to secure her more honour than was absolutely necessary for executing all that He had charged her with. Christ our Saviour yielded to this most prudent petition of His mother, reserving to Himself the duty of spreading the knowledge of her at a more convenient and opportune time; yet in secret He conferred upon her new extraordinary favours.

3. With this little flock our divine shepherd Jesus left the Cenacle, and, with His most blessed mother at His side, He conducted them all through the streets of Jerusalem. The apostles and all the rest in their order, proceeded in the direction of Bethany, which was less than half a league over the brow of mount Olivet. The company of angels and saints from Limbo and Purgatory followed the Victor with new songs of praise, although Mary alone was privileged to see them. The Resurrection of Jesus of Nazareth was already divulged throughout Jerusalem and Palestine. Although the perfidious and malicious princes and priests had spread about the false testimony of His being stolen by the disciples, yet many would not accept their testimony, nor give it any credit. It was divinely provided, that none of the inhabitants of the city, and none of the unbelievers or doubters, should pay any attention to this holy procession, or hinder it on its way from the Cenacle. All, except the one hundred and twenty just, who were chosen by the Lord to witness His Ascension into heaven, were justly punished by being prevented from noticing this wonderful mystery, and the Chieftain and Head of this procession remained invisible to them.

4. The Lord having thus secured them this privacy, they all ascended mount Olivet to its highest point. There they formed three choirs, one of the angels, another of the saints, and a third of the apostles and faithful, which again divided into two bands, while Christ the Saviour presided. Then the most prudent mother prostrated herself at the feet of her son and, worshipping Him with admirable humility, she adored Him as the true God and as the Redeemer of the

world, asking His last blessing. All the faithful there present imitated her and did the same. Weeping and sighing, they asked the Lord, whether He was now to restore the kingdom of Israel. The Lord answered, that this was a secret of the Eternal Father and not to be made known to them; but, for the present, it was necessary and befitting, that they receive the Holy Spirit and preach, in Jerusalem, in Samaria and in all the world, the mysteries of the Redemption of the world.

5. Jesus, having taken leave of this holy and fortunate gathering of the faithful, His countenance beaming forth peace and majesty, joined His hands and, by His own power, began to raise Himself from the earth, leaving thereon the impression of His sacred feet. In gentlest motion He was carried toward the aerial regions, drawing after Him the eyes and the hearts of those firstborn children, who amid sighs and tears vented their affection. And as, at the moving of the first cause of all motion, it is proper that also the nether spheres should be set in motion, so the Saviour Jesus drew after Him also the celestial choirs of the angels, the holy Patriarchs and the rest of the glorified saints, some of them with body and soul, others only as to their soul. All of them in heavenly order were raised up together from the earth, accompanying and following their King, their Chief and Head.

6. The new and mysterious sign, which the right hand of the Most High performed on this occasion for His most holy mother, was that He raised her up with Him in order to put her in possession of the glory, which He had assigned to her as His true mother and which she had by her merits

prepared and earned for herself. In order that this mystery might be kept secret from all other living creatures at that time, and in order that the heavenly mistress might be present in the gathering of the apostles and the faithful in their prayerful waiting upon the coming of the Holy Spirit, the divine power enabled the blessed mother miraculously to be in two places at once; remaining with the children of the Church for their comfort during their stay in the Cenacle and at the same time ascending with the Redeemer of the world to His heavenly throne, where she remained for three days. There she enjoyed the perfect use of all her powers and faculties, whereas she was more restricted in the use of them during that time in the Cenacle.

7. At their entrance the angels, who had ascended from the earth with their sovereigns Jesus and Mary, and those who had joined them in the aerial regions, spoke to those who had remained in the heavenly heights and repeated those words of David and many others referring to this mystery, saying, "Open, O you princes, open your eternal gates; let them be raised and opened up, and receive into His dwelling the great King of glory, the Lord of virtues, the Powerful in battle, the Strong and Invincible, who comes triumphant and victorious over all His enemies. Open the gates of the heavenly paradise, and let them remain open and free forever, since the new Adam is coming, the Repairer of the whole human race, rich in mercy, overflowing with the merits of His copious Redemption achieved by His glorious sacrifice. He has restored our loss and has raised human nature to the supreme dignity of His own immensity. He comes with the reign of the elect and the redeemed, given to Him by

His Eternal Father. He brings with Him and at His side the mother of piety, who gave Him the form of man for overcoming the demon; she comes as our charming and beautiful Queen delighting all that behold her. Come forth, come forth, O you heavenly courtiers, and you shall see our most beautiful King with the crown given to Him by His mother, and His mother crowned with the glory conferred upon her by her son."

8. On this occasion the humility and wisdom of our most prudent Queen reached their highest point; for, over-whelmed by such divine and admirable favours, she hov-ered at the footstool of the royal throne, annihilated in the consciousness of being a mere earthly creature. Prostrate she adored the Father and broke out in new canticles of praise for the glory communicated to His Son and for elevating in Him the deified humanity to such greatness and splendour. Again the angels and saints were filled with admiration and joy to see the most prudent humility of their Queen, whose living example of virtue, as exhibited on that occasion, they emulated among themselves in cop-ying. Then the voice of the Eternal Father was heard saying, "My Daughter, ascend higher!" Her divine son also called her, saying, "My mother, rise up and take possession of the place, which I owe You for having followed and imitated Me." The Holy Spirit said, "My spouse and Beloved, come to my eternal embraces!" Immediately was proclaimed to all the blessed the decree of the Most Holy Trinity, by which the most blessed mother, for having furnished her own lifeblood toward the Incarnation and for having nourished, served, imitated and followed Him with all the perfection

possible to a creature, was exalted and placed at the right hand of her son for all eternity. None other of the human creatures should ever hold that place or position, nor rival her in the unfailing glory connected with it; but it was to be reserved to the Queen and to be her possession by right after her earthly life, as of one who pre-eminently excelled all the rest of the saints.

9. The faithful disciples and holy women had been left in sorrow on mount Olivet, but the most holy Mary did not forget them in the midst of her glory; as they stood weeping and lost in grief and, as it were, absorbed in looking into the aerial regions, into which their Redeemer and Master had disappeared, she turned her eyes upon them from the cloud on which she had ascended, in order to send them her assistance. Moved by their sorrow, she besought Jesus lovingly to console these little children, whom He had left as orphans upon the earth. Moved by the prayers of His mother, the Redeemer of the human race sent down two angels in white and resplendent garments, who appeared to all the disciples and the faithful and spoke to them, "Men of Galilee, do not look up to heaven in so great astonishment, for this Lord Jesus, who departed from you and has ascended into heaven, shall again return with the same glory and majesty in which you have just seen Him." By such words and others which they added they consoled the apostles and disciples and all the rest, so that they might not grow faint, but, in their retirement, hope for the coming and the consolation of the Holy Spirit promised by their Divine Master.

10. These words of the angels, though they consoled these men and women, at the same time contained a reproach of their lack of faith. If their faith had been well founded and permeated by the pure love and charity, it would not have been necessary to remain there with their gaze so intently fixed on the heavens. They should have enlivened their faith and looked for Him and sought Him there, where He really was and where they would certainly have found Him. If their Divine Master had not left them by ascending into heaven, they could not have separated from Him without great bitterness and sorrow, and therefore would not have been as fit to preach the Gospel; for this was to be preached throughout the world at the cost of much labours and difficulties, and at the risk of life itself. This could not be the work of small-minded men, but of men courageous and strong in love, men not hampered or softened by the sensible delights clinging to the spirit, but ready to go through abundance or want, infamy or renown, honours or dishonours, sorrows or joys, preserving throughout it all their love and zeal for the Lord, and a magnanimous heart, superior to all prosperity and adversity. After they had therefore been admonished by the angels they left mount Olivet and returned to the Cenacle with most holy Mary, persevering in prayer and in their expectation of the coming of the Holy Spirit.

GLORY BE TO THE FATHER   Glory be to the Father, and to the Son, and to the Holy Spirit, as it was in the beginning, is now and ever shall be, world without end. Amen.

THE FATIMA PRAYER   O my Jesus, forgive us our sins, save us from the fires of hell, lead all souls to heaven, especially those in most need of Thy mercy.

The Descent of the Holy Spirit

THE FRUIT OF THIS MYSTERY

Perfect docility to the promptings of the Holy Spirit

N THE COMPANY OF the great Queen of heaven, and encouraged by her, the twelve apostles and the rest of the disciples and faithful joyfully waited for the fulfilment of the promise of the Saviour, that He would send them the Holy Spirit, the Consoler, who should instruct them and administer unto them all that they had heard in the teaching of their Lord. They were so unanimous and united in charity, that during all these days none of them had any thought, affection or inclination contrary to those of the rest. They were of one heart and soul in thought and action. Although the election of saint Mathias had occurred, not the least movement or sign of discord arose among all those first-born children of the Church; yet this was a transaction, which is otherwise apt to arouse differences of opinion in the most excellently disposed; since each one is apt to follow his own insight and does not easily yield to the opinion of others. But into this holy congregation no discord found entrance, because they were united in prayer, in fasting and in the expectation of the Holy Spirit, who does not seek repose in discordant and unyielding hearts. In order that it may be inferred, how powerful was this union in charity, not only for disposing them toward the reception of the Holy Spirit, but for overcoming and dispersing the evil spirits, I will say; that the demons, who since the death of the Saviour had lain prostrate in hell, felt in themselves a new kind of oppression and terror, resulting from the virtues of those assembled in the Cenacle. Although they could not explain it to themselves, they perceived a new terrifying force, emanating from that place, and when they perceived the effects of the doctrine and example of Christ in the behaviour of the disciples, they feared the ruin of their dominion.

OUR FATHER   Our Father, Who art in Heaven, hallowed be Thy name, Thy kingdom come, Thy will be done, on earth as it is in heaven. Give us this day our daily bread; and forgive us our trespasses, as we forgive those who trespass against us; and lead us not into temptation, but deliver us from evil. Amen.

HAIL MARY (10)   Hail Mary, Full of Grace, the Lord is with thee. Blessed art thou among women and blessed is the fruit of thy womb, Jesus. Holy Mary, mother of God, pray for us sinners now, and at the hour of our death. Amen.

1. Mary was three days in heaven enjoying the beatific vision and she came back from her heavenly seat on the day which corresponds to the Sunday after the day of the Ascension. She remained in the Cenacle three succeeding days enjoying the after-effects of the beatific vision. During this time the heavenly splendours, which still clothed her, were tempered and only the Evangelist saint John had full knowledge of the mystery; for it was not opportune that it should become known to the rest of the apostles at that time, because they were scarcely as yet capable of such wonders. This miracle of Mary's admission into heaven does not conflict with what is written in the Acts of the Apostles, for St. Luke writes his history according to what he and the apostles saw in the Cenacle of Jerusalem, and irrespective of the mystery of which they were ignorant. The sacred body of Mary was in two places at the same time. Although the attention and use of the senses and faculties was more perfect and real in heaven, nevertheless it could be truly said, that she was in the company of the apostles and that she was seen by all. Moreover it was true that the most blessed Mary persevered with them in prayer; for she saw them from her place in heaven and there she united her prayers and petitions with those of all the holy refugees of the Cenacle; she presented

them to her divine son, at whose right hand she was seated, and obtained for them perseverance and many other great favours of the Most High.

2. The most fortunate apostle saint John saw her ascend and seated at the right hand of her son; he also saw her descend, as I have said, with renewed astonishment. The mysteries of this vision remained impressed upon the memory of saint John, so that neither these, nor all the others revealed to him by the Queen of the angels, ever escaped his mind. But the humility of the most prudent Mary our lady deterred him as long as she lived and persuaded him to keep them hidden within his bosom until the Most High should command otherwise; for it was not opportune to manifest them to the world beforehand. The apostle obeyed the wishes of the heavenly mother and only disclosed the mystery under the metaphors of the book of the Apocalypse; especially by introducing the most holy Mary under the type of the holy Jerusalem, thus saint John says, "I saw the holy city of the new Jerusalem, prepared and adorned as a bride, descending from heaven." There is no doubt that this metaphor of the city refers truly to the most holy Mary, and points out her descent after having ascended with her most blessed Son. The text further states, "And I heard a great voice from the throne, saying, 'Behold the tabernacle of God with men, and He will dwell with them. And they shall be His people; and God Himself with them shall be their God.'"

3. The vigilant mother, empowered by the right hand of her divine son, took care of that happy family in order to bring all their works up to the highest perfection. After her

descent from heaven, she instructed the apostles, yet she never entered upon this duty without first being requested by saint Peter or saint John. Through her prayers she moved her divine son to inspire them with these commands, in order that she might obey them as His vicars and priests. Thus all things happened as arranged by the mother of humility and she obeyed as a handmaid. Laying aside all pretence to her dignity as Queen and lady, and making no use of her sovereignty and dominion, she obeyed as a servant and conducted herself as if she were an inferior, and in this spirit she conferred with the apostles and the other faithful. During those days she explained to them the mystery of the Blessed Trinity in terms most exalted and mysterious, yet suited to the understanding of all. She explained also the mystery of the hypostatic union, and those of the Incarnation, adding many others, which they had already been taught by the Master; telling them at the same time that they would be enlightened by the Holy Spirit for a deeper understanding of all these things.

4. The Queen of the angels, most holy Mary, in the plenitude of her wisdom and grace, knew the time and predestined hour for the sending of the Holy Spirit upon the apostolic college. When the days of Pentecost were about to be fulfilled, the most blessed mother saw in heaven the humanity of the Word conferring with the Eternal Father concerning the promised sending of the divine Paraclete to the apostles, and that the time predetermined by His infinite wisdom for planting the faith and all His gifts in His holy Church, was at hand. He besought His Father also, that, besides bringing grace and the invisible gifts, the Holy Spirit appear

in the world in visible form, that so the evangelical law might be honoured before all the world; that the apostles and faithful, who were to spread the divine truth, might be encouraged, and that the enemies of the Lord, who had in this life persecuted and despised Him unto the death of the cross, might be filled with terror.

5. This petition of our Redeemer in heaven was supported on earth by most holy Mary in a manner befitting the merciful mother of the faithful. Prostrate upon the earth in the form of a cross and in profoundest humility, she saw, how in that consistory of the Blessed Trinity, the request of the Saviour was favourably accepted, and how, to fulfil and execute it, the Persons of the Father and the Son, as the Principle from which the Holy Spirit proceeded, decreed the active mission of the Holy Spirit; for to these Two is attributed the sending of the third Person, because He proceeds from Both; and the third Person passively took upon Himself this mission and consented to come into the world.

6. On Pentecost morning the blessed Virgin Mary exhorted the apostles, the disciples and the pious women, numbering about one hundred and twenty, to pray more fervently and renew their hopes, since the hour was at hand in which they were to be visited by the Divine Spirit from on high. At the third hour, when all of them were gathered around their heavenly mistress and engaged in fervent prayer, the air resounded with a tremendous thunder and the blowing of a violent wind mixed with the brightness of fire or lightning, all centring upon the house of the Cenacle. The house was enveloped in light and the divine fire was poured

out over all of that holy gathering. Over the head of each of the hundred and twenty persons appeared a tongue of that same fire, in which the Holy Spirit had come, filling each one with divine influences and heavenly gifts and causing at one and the same time the most diverse and contrary effects in the Cenacle and in the whole of Jerusalem, according to the diversity of the persons affected.

7. In the most holy Mary these effects were altogether divine, and most wonderful in the sight of all the heavenly courtiers; for as regard us men, we are incapable of understanding and explaining them. The purest lady was transformed and exalted in God; for she saw intuitively and clearly the Holy Spirit, and for a short time enjoyed the beatific vision of the Divinity. Of His gifts and divine influences she by herself received more than all the rest of the saints. Her glory for that space of time, exceeded that of the angels and of the blessed. She alone gave to the Lord more glory, praise and thanksgiving than all the universe for the benefit of the descent of His Holy Spirit upon His Church and for His having pledged Himself so many times to send Him and through Him to govern it to the end of the world. The Blessed Trinity was so pleased with the conduct of Mary on this occasion, that It considered Itself fully repaid and compensated for having created the world; and not only compensated, but God acted as if He were under a certain obligation for possessing such a peerless Creature, whom the Father could look upon as His daughter, the Son as His mother, and the Holy Spirit as His spouse; and whom, according to our way of thinking, He was now obliged to visit and enrich after having conferred upon her such high

dignity. In this exalted and blessed spouse were renewed all the gifts and graces of the Holy Spirit, creating new effects and operations altogether beyond our capacity to understand.

8. The apostles were also replenished and filled with the Holy Spirit; for they received a wonderful increase of justifying grace of a most exalted degree. The twelve apostles were confirmed in this sanctifying grace and were never to lose it. In all of them, according to each one's condition, were infused the habits of the seven gifts. In this magnificent blessing, as new as it was admirable in the world, the twelve apostles were created fit ministers of the New Testament and founders of the Church for the whole world, for this new grace and blessing communicated to them a divine strength most efficacious and sweet, which inclined them to practice the most heroic virtue and the highest sanctity. Thus strengthened they prayed, they laboured willingly and accomplished the most difficult and arduous tasks, engaging in their labours not with sorrow or from necessity, but with the greatest joy and alacrity.

9. In all the rest of the disciples and the faithful who received the Holy Spirit, the Most High brought about proportionally similar effects. According to the disposition of each the gifts of grace were communicated in greater or less abundance in view of the ministry they were to hold in the holy Church. The same proportion was maintained in regard to the apostles; yet saint Peter and saint John were more singularly favoured on account of the high offices assigned to them, the one to govern the Church as its head, and the other to attend upon and serve the Queen and mistress

of heaven and of earth, most holy Mary. The Holy Spirit filled the whole house in which this happy congregation was gathered, not only because all of them were filled with the Holy Spirit and His admirable gifts, but because the house itself was filled with wonderful light and splendour. This plenitude of wonders and prodigies overflowed and communicated itself also to others outside of the Cenacle; for it caused diverse and various effects of the Holy Spirit among the inhabitants of Jerusalem and its vicinity. All those who with some piety had sorrowed over our Saviour Jesus in His passion and death were now converted by the first sermon of saint Peter.

10. Not less wonderful, although more hidden, were some contrary effects produced on that day by the Holy Spirit in Jerusalem. By the dreadful thunders and violent commotion of the atmosphere and the lightnings accompanying His advent, He disturbed and terrified the enemies of the Lord in that city, each one according to his own malice and perfidy. This chastisement was particularly evident in those who had actively concurred in procuring the death of Christ, and who had signalised themselves in their rabid fury against Him. All these fell to the ground on their faces and remained thus for three hours. Those that had scourged the Lord were suddenly choked in their own blood, which shot forth from their veins in punishment for shedding that of the Master. The audacious servant, who had buffeted the Lord, not only suddenly died, but was hurled into hell body and soul. Others of the Jews, although they did not die, were chastised with intense pains and abominable sicknesses. These disorders, consequent upon shedding the blood of Christ,

descended to their posterity and even to this day continue to afflict their children with most horrible impurities. This chastisement became notorious in Jerusalem, although the priests and Pharisees diligently sought to cover it up, just as they had tried to conceal the Resurrection of the Saviour. As these events, however, were not so important, neither the apostles nor the Evangelists wrote about them, and in the confusion of the city the multitude soon forgot them.

GLORY BE TO THE FATHER   Glory be to the Father, and to the Son, and to the Holy Spirit, as it was in the beginning, is now and ever shall be, world without end. Amen.

THE FATIMA PRAYER   O my Jesus, forgive us our sins, save us from the fires of hell, lead all souls to heaven, especially those in most need of Thy mercy.

The Assumption of the Blessed Virgin

THE FRUIT OF THIS MYSTERY

A desire to communicate Our Lady's virtues and privileges to others

HE BLESSED VIRGIN'S MOST pure soul passed from her virginal body to be placed in boundless glory, on the throne at the right hand of her divine son. Immediately the music of the angels seemed to withdraw to the upper air; for that whole procession of angels and saints accompanied the King and Queen to the empyrean heavens. The sacred body of the most blessed Mary, which had been the temple and sanctuary of God in life, continued to shine with an effulgent light and breathed forth such a wonderful and unheard of fragrance, that all the bystanders were filled with interior and exterior sweetness. The thousand angels of her guard remained to watch over the inestimable treasure of her virginal body. The apostles and disciples, amid the tears and the joy of the wonders they had seen, were absorbed in admiration for some time, and then sang many hymns and psalms in honour of the most blessed Mary now departed. This glorious Transition of the great Queen took place in the hour in which her divine son had died, at three o'clock on a Friday, the thirteenth day of August, she being seventy years of age. Great wonders and prodigies happened at the precious death of the Queen; for the sun was eclipsed and its light was hidden in sorrow for some hours. Many birds of different kinds gathered around the Cenacle, and by their sorrowful clamours and groans for a while caused the bystanders themselves to weep. All Jerusalem was in commotion, and many of the inhabitants collected in astonished crowds, confessing loudly the power of God and the greatness of His works. Others were astounded and as if beside themselves. The apostles and disciples with others of the faithful broke forth in tears and sighs. Many sick persons who had come were cured. Souls in Purgatory were released.

OUR FATHER   Our Father, Who art in Heaven, hallowed be Thy name, Thy kingdom come, Thy will be done, on earth as it is in heaven. Give us this day our daily bread; and forgive us our trespasses, as we forgive those who trespass against us; and lead us not into temptation, but deliver us from evil. Amen.

HAIL MARY (10)   Hail Mary, Full of Grace, the Lord is with thee. Blessed art thou among women and blessed is the fruit of thy womb, Jesus. Holy Mary, mother of God, pray for us sinners now, and at the hour of our death. Amen.

1. The evangelist saint John made preparations for the journey and embarkation for Ephesus, and on the fourth day, which was the fifth of January of the year forty, saint John notified her that it was time to leave; for there would be a ship and all things had been arranged for the journey. The great Queen of the world was now for the first time upon the sea. She saw and comprehended with clearness the vast Mediterranean and its communication with the great ocean. She beheld its height and depth, its length and breadth, its caverns and secret recesses, its sands and minerals, its ebb and tide, its animals, its whales and fish of all sizes, and whatever other wonderful animals it enclosed. When this great panorama of creatures was presented to her, she was filled with heavenly wisdom, and praised Almighty God, Who she saw as so wonderfully reflected in those creatures. With the compassion of a most loving mother for those who live their lives at sea, she most fervently besought the Almighty to protect from its dangers all who should call upon her name and ask for her intercession. The Lord immediately granted this petition and promised to favour whoever upon the sea should carry some image of her and

should sincerely look upon this Star of the Sea, most blessed Mary, for help in its perils.

2. The most holy Mary had arrived at the age of sixty-seven years without having mitigated the flame of her love, or lessened the increase of her merits from the first instant of her conception. Now, however, the bounds of her flesh were becoming most violently irksome; the overwhelming attraction of the Divinity to unite Itself with her had attained the summit of power in her; and the earth itself, made unworthy by the sins of mortals to contain the treasure of heaven, could no longer bear the strain of withholding her from her true Lord. The Eternal Father desired His only and true daughter; the Son His beloved and most loving mother; and the Holy Spirit the embraces of His most beautiful spouse. The angels longed for their Queen, the saints for their great lady; and all the heavens mutely awaited the presence of their Empress who should fill them with glory, with her beauty and delight. All that could be alleged in favour of her still remaining in the world and in the Church, was the need of such a mother and mistress, and the love, which God Himself had for the miserable children of Adam.

3. The Almighty therefore resolved to delight and console her by giving her definite notice of the term still remaining of her life and revealing to her the day and hour of the longed for end of her earthly banishment. For this pur-pose the most Blessed Trinity dispatched the Archangel Gabriel with many others of the celestial hierarchies, who should announce to the Queen when and how her mortal

life should come to an end and pass over into the eternal. The holy prince descended with the rest to the Cenacle in Jerusalem and entered the oratory of the great lady, where they found her prostrate on the ground in the form of a cross, asking mercy for sinners. But hearing the sound of their music and perceiving them present, she rose to her knees in order to hear the message and show respect to the ambassador of heaven and his companions, who in white and refulgent garments surrounded her with wonderful delight and reverence. All of them had come with crowns and palms in their hands, each with a different one; but all of them represented the diverse tributes and rewards of inestimable beauty and value to be conferred upon their great Queen and lady. Gabriel saluted her with the Ave Maria, and added, "Our Empress and lady, the Omnipotent and the Holy of the Holy sends us from His heavenly court to announce to You in His name the most happy end of your pilgrimage and banishment upon earth in mortal life. Soon, O lady, is that day and hour approaching, in which, according to your longing desires, you shall pass through natural death to the possession of the eternal and immortal life, which awaits you in the glory and at the right hand of your divine Son, our God. Exactly three years from today you shall be taken up and received into the everlasting joy of the Lord, where all its inhabitants await you, longing for your presence."

4. During the course of these three last years of the life of our Queen and lady the divine power permitted a certain hidden and sweet force to throw all nature into mourning and sorrow at the prospective death of her, who by her life

beautified and perfected all creation. The holy apostles, although they were scattered over the earth, began to feel new anxiety and misgivings regarding the time when they should be deprived of their mistress and her help; for already the divine light intimated to them, that this event could not be far off. The others of the faithful living in Jerusalem and in the country around, began secretly to feel that their treasure and joy should not be theirs much longer. The heavens, the stars and planets lost much of their brightness and beauty, like the day at the approach of night. The birds of the air fell into singular demonstrations of sorrow during these last years. A great multitude of them ordinarily gathered where the most blessed Mary happened to be. Surrounding her oratory in unusual flight and motions, they uttered, instead of their natural songs, sorrowful notes, as if they were lamenting and groaning in their grief, until the lady herself ordered them again to praise their Creator in their natural and musical tones. Of this miracle saint John was often a witness, joining them in their lamentations. A few days before the transition of the heavenly mother innumerable hosts of the little birds gathered, laying their heads and beaks upon the ground, picking at their breasts in groans, like some one taking farewell forever and asking the last blessing.

5. And now, according to the decree of the divine will, the day was approaching in which the true and living Ark of the Covenant was to be placed in the temple of the celestial Jerusalem, with a greater glory and higher jubilee than its prophetic figure was installed by Solomon in the sanctuary beneath the wings of the cherubim. Three days before the

most happy transition of the great lady the apostles and disciples were gathered in Jerusalem and in the Cenacle. The first one to arrive was saint Peter, who was transported from Rome by the hands of an angel. At that place the angel appeared to him and told him that the passing away of the most blessed Mary was imminent and that the Lord commanded him to go to Jerusalem in order to be present at that event. Thereupon the angel took him up and brought him from Italy to the Cenacle. To there the Queen of the World had retired, somewhat weakened in body by the force of her divine love; for since she was so near to her end, she was subjected more completely to love's effects. Some of the apostles who had been transported by the angels and informed by them of the purpose of their coming, were seized with tenderest grief and shed abundant tears at the thought of losing their only protection and consolation. Others were as yet ignorant of their approaching loss, especially the disciples, who had not been positively informed by the angels, but were moved by interior inspirations and a sweet and forcible intimation of God's will to come to Jerusalem. They immediately conferred with saint Peter, desirous of knowing the occasion of their meeting; for all of them were convinced, that if there had been no special occasion, the Lord would not have urged them so strongly to come. The apostle saint Peter, as the head of the Church, called them all together in order to tell them of the cause of their coming, and spoke to the assembly, "My dearest children and brethren, the Lord has called and brought us to Jerusalem from remote regions not without a cause most urgent and sorrowful to us. The Most High wishes now to raise up to the throne of eternal glory His most blessed mother, our mistress, our consolation and protection. His divine decree is that we all be present at her most happy and glorious transition. When our Master and Redeemer ascended to the right hand of His Father, although He left us orphaned of His most delightful presence, we still retained His most blessed mother. As our light now leaves us, what shall we do? What help or hope have we to encourage us on our pilgrimage? I find none except the hope that we all shall follow her in due time."

6. The sweetest mother proceeded in her leave-taking, speaking to each of the apostles in particular and to some of the disciples; and then to all the assembly together; for there were a great number. The words of the most blessed Mary, like arrows of a divine fire, penetrated the hearts of all the apostles and hearers, and as she ceased speaking, all of them were dissolved in streams of tears and, seized with irreparable sorrow, cast themselves upon the ground with sighs and groans sufficient to move to compassion the very earth. All of them wept, and with them wept also the sweetest Mary, who could not resist this bitter and well-founded sorrow of her children. After some time she spoke to them again, and asked them to pray with her and for her in silence, which they did. During this quietness the Incarnate Word descended from heaven on a throne of ineffable glory, accompanied by all the saints and innumerable angels, and the house of the Cenacle was filled with glory. The most blessed Mary adored the Lord and kissed His feet. Prostrate before Him she made the last and most profound act of faith and humility in her mortal life. The most prudent mother prostrated herself at the feet of her son and with a joyous

countenance answered, "My son and my Lord, I beseech You let Your mother and Your servant enter into eternal life by the common portal of natural death, like the other children of Adam. You, who are my true God, have suffered death without being obliged to do so; it is proper that, as I have followed You in life, so I follow You also in death."

7. Christ the Saviour approved of the decision and the sacrifice of His most blessed mother, and consented to its fulfilment. Then all the angels began to sing in celestial harmony some of the verses of the Canticles of Solomon and other new ones. Although only saint John and some of the apostles were enlightened as to the presence of Christ the Saviour, yet the others felt in their interior its divine and powerful effects; but the music was heard as well by the apostles and disciples, as by many others of the faithful there present. A divine fragrance also spread about, which penetrated even to the street. The house of the Cenacle was filled with a wonderful effulgence, visible to all, and the Lord ordained that multitudes of the people of Jerusalem gathered in the streets as witnesses to this new miracle. When the angels began their music, the most blessed Mary reclined back upon her couch or bed. Her tunic was folded about her sacred body, her hands were joined and her eyes fixed upon her divine son, and she was entirely inflamed with the fire of divine love. And as the angels intoned those verses of the second chapter of the Canticles, "Arise, haste, my beloved, my dove, my beautiful one, and come, the winter has passed," she pronounced those words of her son on the cross, "Into your hands, O Lord, I commend my spirit." Then she closed her virginal eyes and expired.

The sickness which took away her life was love, without any other weakness or accidental intervention of whatever kind. She died at the moment when the divine power suspended the assistance, which until then had counteracted the sensible ardour of her burning love of God. As soon as this miraculous assistance was withdrawn, the fire of her love consumed her heart and thus caused the cessation of her earthly existence.

8. The holy apostles called the two maidens who had assisted the Queen during her life and instructed them to anoint the body of the Mother of God with highest reverence and modesty and to wrap it in the winding-sheets before it should be placed in the casket. With great reverence and fear the two maidens entered the room, where the body of the blessed lady lay upon its couch; but the refulgence issuing from it barred and blinded them in such a manner that they could neither see nor touch the body, nor even ascertain in what particular place it rested. The apostles, having thus been informed of the will of God, brought a bier, and, the effulgence having diminished somewhat, they approached the couch and with their own hands reverently took hold of the tunic at the two ends. Thus, without changing its posture, they raised the sacred and virginal treasure and placed it on the bier in the same position as it had occupied on the couch. They could easily do this, because they felt no more weight than that of the tunic. On this bier the former effulgence of the body moderated still more, and all of them, by disposition of the Lord and for the consolation of all those present, could now perceive and study the beauty of that virginal countenance and of her hands. As for the

rest, the omnipotence of God protected this His heavenly dwelling, so that neither in life nor in death anyone should behold any other part except what is common in ordinary conversation, namely, her most inspiring countenance, by which she had been known, and her hands, by which she had laboured.

9. When the procession came to the holy sepulchre in the valley of Josaphat, the same two apostles, saint Peter and saint John, who had laid the celestial treasure from the couch onto the bier, with joyful reverence placed it in the sepulchre and covered it with a linen cloth, the hands of the angels performing more of these last rites than the hands of the apostles. They closed up the sepulchre with a large stone, according to custom at other burials. The celestial courtiers returned to heaven, while the thousand angels of the Queen continued their watch, guarding the sacred body and keeping up the music as at her burial. The concourse of the people lessened and the holy apostles and disciples, dissolved in tender tears, returned to the Cenacle. During a whole year the exquisite fragrance exhaled by the body of the Queen was noticeable throughout the Cenacle, and in her oratory, for many years. Having again gathered in the Cenacle, the apostles came to the conclusion that some of them and of the disciples should watch at the sepulchre of their Queen as long as they should hear the celestial music, for all of them were wondering when the end of that miracle should be. Nor were the irrational creatures missing at the funeral services of the mistress of the universe; for as the sacred body arrived near the grave, innumerable large and small birds gathered in the air, and many animals and wild

beasts rushed from the mountains toward the sepulchre, the ones singing sorrowfully the others emitting groans and doleful sounds and all of them showing grief in their movements as if mourning over the common loss. Only a few unbelieving Jews, more hardened than the rocks and more impious than the wild beasts failed to show sorrow at the death of their Restoratrix, as they had failed to do also at the death of their Redeemer and Master.

10. On the third day after the most pure soul of Mary had taken possession of this glory never to leave it, the Lord manifested to the saints His divine will, that she should return to the world, resuscitate her sacred body and unite herself with it, so that she might in body and soul be again raised to the right hand of her divine son without waiting for the general resurrection of the dead. All the ancient saints of the human race then gave thanks for this new favour in songs of praise and glory to the Lord. Those that especially distinguished themselves in their thanksgiving were our first parents Adam and Eve, saint Ann, saint Joachim and saint Joseph, as being the more close partakers in this miracle of His Omnipotence. Then the purest soul of the Queen, at the command of the Lord, entered the virginal body, reanimated it and raised it up, giving it a new life of immortality and glory and communicating to it the four gifts of clearness, impassibility, agility and subtlety, corresponding to those of the soul and overflowing from it into the body. Endowed with these gifts the most blessed Mary issued from the tomb in body and soul, without raising the stone cover and without disturbing the position of the tunic and the mantle that had enveloped her sacred body. Since

it is impossible to describe her beauty and refulgent glory, I will not make the attempt. It is sufficient to say, that just as the heavenly mother had given to her divine son in her womb the form of man, pure, unstained and sinless, for the Redemption of the world, so in return the Lord, in this resurrection and new regeneration, gave to her a glory and beauty similar to His own. In this mysterious and divine interchange each one did what was possible, most holy Mary engendered Christ, assimilating Him as much as possible to herself, and Christ resuscitated her, communicating to her of His glory as far as she was capable as a creature. Then from the sepulchre was started a most solemn procession, moving with celestial music through the regions of the air and toward the empyrean heaven. This happened in the hour immediately after midnight, in which also the Lord had risen from the grave; and therefore not all of the apostles were witness of this prodigy, but only some of them, who were present and watching at the sepulchre.

GLORY BE TO THE FATHER   Glory be to the Father, and to the Son, and to the Holy Spirit, as it was in the beginning, is now and ever shall be, world without end. Amen.

THE FATIMA PRAYER   O my Jesus, forgive us our sins, save us from the fires of hell, lead all souls to heaven, especially those in most need of Thy mercy.

The Coronation of the Blessed Virgin Mary and the Glory of all the Angels and Saints

THE FRUIT OF THIS MYSTERY

Freedom from all worry about things of this passing life

 MID GREAT GLORY THE most holy Mary arrived body and soul at the throne of the most Blessed Trinity. The Eternal Father said to her, "Ascend higher, My daughter and My dove." The Incarnate Word spoke, "My mother, of whom I have received human being and full return of My work in your perfect imitation, receive now from My hand the reward you have merited." The Holy Spirit said, "My most beloved spouse, enter into the eternal joy, which corresponds to the most faithful love; now enjoy your love without solicitude; for past is the winter of suffering for you have arrived at Our eternal embraces." There the most blessed Mary was absorbed in the contemplation of the three divine Persons and as it were overwhelmed in the boundless ocean and abyss of the Divinity, while the saints were filled with wonder and delight.

OUR FATHER   Our Father, Who art in Heaven, hallowed be Thy name, Thy kingdom come, Thy will be done, on earth as it is in heaven. Give us this day our daily bread; and forgive us our trespasses, as we forgive those who trespass against us; and lead us not into temptation, but deliver us from evil. Amen.

HAIL MARY (10)   Hail Mary, Full of Grace, the Lord is with thee. Blessed art thou among women and blessed is the fruit of thy womb, Jesus. Holy Mary, mother of God, pray for us sinners now, and at the hour of our death. Amen.

1. The saints and angels entered heaven in the order in which they had started; and in the last place came Christ our Saviour and at His right hand the Queen, clothed in the gold of variety, and so beautiful that she was the admiration of the heavenly court. All of them turned toward her to look upon her and bless her with new jubilee and songs of

praise. Thus were heard those mysterious eulogies recorded by Solomon, "Come, daughters of Sion, to see your Queen, who is praised by the morning stars and celebrated by the sons of the Most High", "Who is she that comes from the desert, like a column of aromatic perfumes?", "Who is she that comes forth as the morning rising, fair as the moon, bright as the sun, terrible as an army set in battle array?", "Who is she that comes up from the desert resting upon her Beloved and spreading forth abundant delights?" O sight worthy of the infinite Wisdom! O prodigy of His Omnipotence, which so magnifies and exalts her!

2. Amid this glory the most blessed Mary arrived body and soul at the throne of the most Blessed Trinity. The Lord declared to the courtiers of heaven all the privileges she should enjoy in virtue of this participation in His majesty. The Person of the Eternal Father, as the first principle of all things, speaking to the angels and saints, said to them, "Our Daughter Mary was chosen according to Our pleasure from amongst all creatures, the first one to delight Us, and who never fell from the title and position of a true daughter, such as We had given her in Our divine mind; she has a claim on Our dominion, which We shall recognise by crowning her as the legitimate and peerless lady and Sovereign." The Incarnate Word said, "To My true and natural mother belong all the creatures which were created and redeemed my Me; and of all things over which I am King, she too shall be the legitimate and supreme Queen." The Holy Spirit said, "Since she is called My beloved and chosen spouse, she deserves to be crowned as Queen for all eternity."

3. Having thus spoken the three divine Persons placed upon the head of the most blessed Mary a crown of such new splendour and value, that the like has been seen neither before nor after by any mere creature. At the same time a voice sounded from the throne saying, "My Beloved, chosen among the creatures, our kingdom is yours; you shall be the lady and the Sovereign of the seraphim, of all the ministering spirits, the angels and of the entire universe of creatures. Attend, proceed and govern prosperously over them, for in our supreme consistory We give you power, majesty and sovereignty. Being filled with grace beyond all the rest, you have humiliated yourself in your own estimation to the lowest place; receive now the supreme dignity deserved by you and, as a participation in Our Divinity, the dominion over all the creatures of Our Omnipotence. From your royal throne to the centre of the earth you shall reign; and by the power We now give You You shall subject hell with all its demons and inhabitants. Let all of them fear you as the supreme Empress and mistress of those caverns and dwelling-places of our enemies. In your hands and at your pleasure We place the influences and forces of the heavens, the moisture of the clouds, the growths of the earth; and of all of them do you distribute according to your will, and our own will shall be at your disposal for the execution of your wishes. You shall be the Empress and mistress of the militant Church, its Protectress, its Advocate, its mother and Teacher. You shall be the special Patroness of the Catholic countries; and whenever they, or the faithful, or any of the children of Adam call upon you from their heart, serve or oblige you, you shall relieve and help them in their labours and necessities. You shall be the Friend and the Defender of

all the just and of our friends; all of them you shall comfort, console and fill with blessings according to their devotion to you. In view of all this We make you the Depositary of our riches, the treasurer of our goods; We place into your hands the helps and blessings of our grace for distribution; nothing do We wish to be given to the world, which does not pass through your hands; and nothing do We deny, which you wish to concede to men. Grace shall be diffused in your lips for obtaining all that you wish and ordain in heaven and on earth, and everywhere shall angels and men obey you; because whatever is Ours shall be yours, just as you have always been Ours; and you shall reign with Us forever."

4. In the execution of this decree and privilege conceded to the mistress of the world, the Almighty commanded all the courtiers of heaven, angels and men, to show her obedience and recognise her as their Queen and lady. Both the angelic spirits and the blessed souls, while rendering their adoration to the Lord with fear and worshipful reverence, rendered a homage in its proportion to His most blessed mother; and the saints who were there in their bodies prostrated themselves and gave bodily signs of their honour. All these demonstrations at the coronation of the Empress of heaven redounded wonderfully to her glory, to the new joy and jubilee of the saints and to the pleasure of the most Blessed Trinity. Altogether festive was this day, and it produced new glory in all the heavens. Those that partook more especially therein were her most fortunate spouse saint Joseph, saint Joachim and Ann and all the other relatives of the Queen, together with the thousand angels of her guard.

5. Within the glorious body of the Queen, over her heart, was visible to the saints a small globe or monstrance of singular beauty and splendour, which particularly roused and rouses their admiration and joy. It was there in testimony and reward of her having afforded to the sacramental Word an acceptable resting place and sanctuary, and of her having received Holy Communion so worthily, purely and devoutly, without any defect or imperfection, and with a devotion, love and reverence attained by none other of the saints. In regard to the other rewards and crowns corresponding to her peerless works and virtues, nothing that can be said could give any idea; and therefore I refer it to the beatific vision, where each one shall perceive them in proportion as his doings and his devotion shall have merited.

6. We now return to the apostles and disciples, who in flowing tears surrounded the sepulchre of Mary in the valley of Josaphat. Saint Peter and saint John, who had been the most constant in their attendance, noticed that the celestial music had ceased; for they failed to hear it on the third day. Partly enlightened by the Holy Spirit, they conjectured that the most pure mother had arisen and had entered heaven, body and soul, like her divine son. They conferred about this matter and came to the conclusion that so it must be; and saint Peter, as the head of the Church, decided that such a wonderful fact should be ascertained as far as possible and made known to those who had witnessed her death and burial. For this purpose, on the same day, he called together the apostles, disciples and the other faithful at the sepulchre. He told them of his reasons for the conjecture now in the mind of all and the reasons for manifesting the

truth of this wonder to the Church, namely, that it should be reverenced in the coming ages and would redound to the glory of the Lord and of His most blessed mother. All approved of the decision of the vicar of Christ and at his order immediately removed the stone, which closed the sepulchre. This being done, they saw the grave empty of the sacred body of the Queen of heaven and the tunic in the same position as when it had covered her, showing that it must have passed through the tunic and the stone of the sepulchre without disturbing any part of them. Saint Peter took out the tunic and the mantle and, with all the others, venerated it, as they were now certain of the Resurrection and Assumption of the blessed mother into heaven. In mixed joy and sorrow they wept sweet tears at this prodigy and sang psalms and hymns of praise and glory to the Lord and His most blessed mother.

7. In their affectionate wonder all of them remained looking at the sepulchre, spellbound, until the angel of the Lord descended and manifested himself to them, saying, "Men of Galilee, why are you astounded? Your and our Queen now lives body and soul in heaven and reigns in it forever with Christ. She sends me to confirm you in this truth, and in her name I tell you that she recommends to you anew the Church, the conversion of souls, and the spread of the Gospel. She desires to tell you that you now return to your ministry, with which you were charged, and that from her throne she will take care of you." At this message the apostles were consoled; they experienced her protection in their wanderings, and much more in the hour of their

martyrdom; for to each of them did she appear in that hour to present their souls to the Lord.

8. Our Lady spoke from glory, "My daughter, if anything could lessen the enjoyment of the highest felicity and glory which I possess, and if, in it, I could be capable of any sorrow, without a doubt I would be grieved to see the holy Church and the rest of the world in its present state of labour, notwithstanding that men know me to be their mother, Advocate and Protectress in heaven, ready to guide and assist them to eternal life. In this state of affairs, when the Almighty has granted me so many privileges as His mother and when there are so many sources of help placed in my hands solely for the benefit of mortals and belonging to me as the mother of clemency, it is a great cause of sorrow to me to see mortals force me to remain idle, and that, for want of calling upon me, so many souls should be lost. But if I cannot experience grief now, I may justly complain of men, that they load themselves with eternal damnation and refuse me the glory of saving their souls."

9. "The Most High still wishes to give liberally of His infinite treasures and resolves to favour those who know how to gain my intercession before God. This is the secure way and the powerful means of advancing the Church, of improving the Catholic reigns, of spreading the faith, of furthering the welfare of families and of states, of bringing the souls to grace and to the friendship of God. Consider well, my dearest, your strict obligation of serving me as your only mother, as your legitimate and true Teacher and Superior, who favours you with many graces and condescensions."

10. Just as Almighty God providentially concealed the body and the burial of Moses, whom the Jews esteemed so highly, lest they might begin to venerate him by some superstitious and vain cult, He hid many of the prerogatives of His Holy Mother to these latter days. If, in the first preaching of the Gospel and the faith of Christ our Saviour, the great excellences of His most holy mother had been propounded to the pagan nations, the gentiles would have been great danger of error and confusion. In this danger then would have fallen, much more easily, the ignorant, and they would certainly have confounded the Divinity of Christ the Redeemer, which they were obliged to believe, together with the greatness of His most pure mother, thinking that, since they were propounded at the same time and showed such similarity in holiness, she was a God just as her son. But this danger vanished after the faith and practice of the Church had taken such deep roots and after it had been so clearly established by the teachings of the holy doctors and by so many miracles worked by God in testimony of the Redeemer. Enlightened by these testimonies we know that He alone is God and true man, full of truth and grace; and that His mother is a mere creature, full of grace without possessing the Divinity and yet next to God and above all the rest of creation. In our times then, so enlightened by the divine truths, the Lord has decided to spread the glory of His most holy mother by opening up the enigmas and secrets of the Holy Scriptures wherein He holds them enshrined.

GLORY BE TO THE FATHER   Glory be to the Father, and to the Son, and to the Holy Spirit, as it was in the beginning, is now and ever shall be, world without end. Amen.

THE FATIMA PRAYER   O my Jesus, forgive us our sins, save us from the fires of hell, lead all souls to heaven, especially those in most need of Thy mercy.

CONCLUDING PRAYERS   *Upon completing the recitation of the Holy Rosary, the following prayers are customary, but others too may be added according to one's devotion and preference.*

HAIL HOLY QUEEN   Hail Holy Queen, mother of Mercy, hail our life, our sweetness and our hope. To thee do we cry, poor banished children of Eve, to thee do we send up our sighs, mourning and weeping in this vale of tears. Turn then, most gracious advocate, thine eyes of mercy towards us, and after this, our exile, show unto us the blessed fruit of thy womb, Jesus. O clement, O loving, O sweet Virgin Mary. Pray for us O holy mother of God, that we may be made worthy of the promises of Christ.

Let Us Pray   O God, Whose only begotten son, by His life, death and resurrection, has purchased for us the rewards of eternal life, grant we beseech Thee, that meditating on these mysteries of the most Holy Rosary of the Blessed Virgin Mary, we may both imitate what they contain and obtain what they promise, through the same Christ our Lord. Amen.

PRAYER TO SAINT MICHAEL THE ARCHANGEL   Holy Michael, Archangel, defend us in the day of battle. Be our safeguard against the wickedness and snares of the devil. May God rebuke him, we humbly pray; and do thou, O Prince of the heavenly hosts, by the power of God thrust down

into hell Satan and all the evil spirits who wander through the world seeking the ruin of souls. Amen.

MEMORARE   Remember, O most gracious Virgin Mary, that never was it known that anyone who fled to thy protection, implored thy help, or sought thine intercession was left unaided. Inspired by this confidence, I fly unto thee, O Virgin of virgins, my mother; to thee do I come, before you I stand, sinful and sorrowful. O mother of the Word Incarnate, despise not my petitions, but in thy mercy hear and answer me. Amen.

May the Divine Assistance remain always with us, and may the souls of the faithful departed, through the mercy of God rest in peace. Amen.

The Mysteries of Light

The Baptism of Our Lord in the River Jordan

THE FRUIT OF THIS MYSTERY

Joy at being reborn in grace as a child of God

HIS ACT OF HUMILIATION of receiving baptism in the company of those who were sinners, Christ our Redeemer offered up to the Eternal Father as an act of acknowledgment of the inferiority of His human nature, which, in common with all the rest of the children of men, He had derived from Adam. By it He also instituted the sacrament of baptism, which was to wash away the sins of the world through His merits. By thus humiliating Himself in this baptism of sins, He sought and obtained from the Eternal Father a general pardon for all those who were to receive it; He freed them from the power of the demon and of sin, and regenerated them to a new existence, spiritual and supernatural as adopted sons of the Most High, brethren of their Redeemer and Lord.

OUR FATHER   Our Father, Who art in Heaven, hallowed be Thy name, Thy kingdom come, Thy will be done, on earth as it is in heaven. Give us this day our daily bread; and forgive us our trespasses, as we forgive those who trespass against us; and lead us not into temptation, but deliver us from evil. Amen.

HAIL MARY (10)   Hail Mary, Full of Grace, the Lord is with thee. Blessed art thou among women and blessed is the fruit of thy womb, Jesus. Holy Mary, mother of God, pray for us sinners now, and at the hour of our death. Amen.

1. Leaving His beloved mother in the poor dwelling at Nazareth, our Redeemer, without accompaniment of any human creature, but altogether taken up with the exercise of His most ardent charity, pursued His journey to the Jordan, where, in the neighbourhood of a town called Bethany, His Precursor was preaching and baptising. At the first steps from the house, our Redeemer, raising His eyes to the Eternal Father, offered up to Him anew with an infinite love, whatever He was now about to begin for the salvation

of mankind, His labours, sorrows, passion and death of the cross, assumed for them in obedience to the eternal Will. The Lord of all creation walked alone, without show and ostentation of human retinue. The supreme King of kings and Lord of lords was unknown and despised by His own servants, servants so much His own, that they owed their life and preservation entirely to Him. His royal outfit was nothing but the utmost poverty and destitution.

2. While proceeding on His way to the Jordan, our Saviour dispensed His ancient mercies by relieving the necessities of body and soul in many of those whom He encountered at different places. Yet this was always done in secret; for before His baptism He gave no public token of His divine power and His exalted office. Before appearing at the Jordan, He filled the heart of saint John with new light and joy, which changed and elevated his soul. Perceiving these new workings of grace within himself, he reflected upon them full of wonder, saying, "What mystery is this? What presentiments of happiness? From the moment when I recognised the presence of my Lord in the womb of my mother, I have not felt such stirring of my soul as now! Is it possible that He is now happily come, or that the Saviour of the world is now near me?" Upon this enlightenment of the Baptist followed an intellectual vision, wherein he perceived with greater clearness the mystery of the hypostatic union of the person of the Word with the humanity and other mysteries of the Redemption. The Baptist had been instructed in great mysteries when he was commanded to go forth to preach and baptise; yet all of them were manifested to him anew and with greater clearness and abundance on this occasion,

and he was then notified that the Saviour of the World was coming to be baptised.

3. The Lord then joined the multitude and asked baptism of saint John as one of the rest. The Baptist recognised Him and, falling at His feet, hesitated, saying, "I have need of being baptised, and You, Lord, ask baptism of me?" But the Saviour answered, "Suffer it to be so now. For righteousness demands it." By thus hesitating to baptise Christ his Lord and asking Him for baptism instead, he gave evidence that he recognised Him as the true Redeemer. Up to this point he had not seen Christ bodily and could, therefore, deny having known Christ, as is recorded by St. John. Now he knew Christ both by sight and by intellectual vision, and, in knowing Him, he prostrated himself at the feet of his Saviour.

4. When saint John had finished baptising our Lord, the heavens opened and the Holy Spirit descended visibly in the form of a dove upon His head and the voice of His Father was heard, "This is my beloved Son, in whom I am well pleased." Many of the bystanders heard this voice, namely, those who were worthy of such a wonderful favour; they also saw the Holy Spirit descending upon the Saviour. This was the most convincing proof which could ever be given of the Divinity of the Saviour, as well on the part of the Father, who acknowledged Him His Son, as also in regard to the nature of the testimony given; for without any reserve was Christ manifested as the true God, equal to His Eternal Father in substance and in perfection. The Father Himself wished to be the first to testify to the Divinity of Christ in order that by virtue of His testimony all the other witnesses

might be ratified. There was also another mystery in this voice of the Eternal Father, it was as it were a restoration of the honour of His Son before the world and a recompense for His having thus humiliated Himself by receiving the baptism of the remission of sins, though He was entirely free from fault and never could have upon Him the guilt of sin.

5. The past, present and future sins of men always remaining in the sight of the Eternal Father, had prevented the effects of this baptism; but Christ our Lord merited the application of this so easy and delightful remedy, so that the Eternal Father was obliged to accept it in justice as a complete satisfaction according to all the requirements of His equity. Christ was also not deterred from thus securing this remedy by His foreknowledge of the abuse of holy baptism by so many mortals in all ages and of its neglect by innumerable others. All these impediments and hindrances Christ our Lord removed by satisfying for their offences, humiliating Himself and assuming the form of a sinner in His baptism.

6. The great Baptist was the one who reaped the greatest fruit from these wonders of holy baptism; for he not only baptised his Redeemer and Master, saw the Holy Spirit and the celestial light descending upon the Lord together with innumerable angels, heard the voice of the Father and saw many other mysteries by divine revelation, but besides all this, he himself was baptised by the Redeemer. The Gospel indeed says no more than that he asked for it, but at the same time it also does not say that it was denied him; for, without a doubt, Christ after His own baptism, conferred it also on His Precursor and Baptist.

7. The baptism given to John did not remove from him the stain of sin, for this had already been remitted before his birth. The baptism, nonetheless, bestowed upon him the character of a Christian, together with a great plenitude of grace. Later, the Lord also baptised His most holy mother before Baptism's general promulgation, and He, on that occasion, established the form in which baptism was to be administered. These facts were made known to me.

8. As soon as Our Lady's most holy son was baptised, the holy angels who had attended upon their Lord brought her intelligence of all that had happened at the Jordan. To celebrate all these mysteries of Christ's baptism and the public proclamation of His Divinity, the most prudent mother composed new hymns and canticles of praise and of incomparable thanksgiving to the Most High and to the Incarnate Word. All His actions of humility and prayers she imitated, exerting herself by many acts of her own to accompany and follow Him in all of them. With ardent charity she interceded for men, that they might profit by the sacrament of baptism and that it might be administered all over the world. In addition to these prayers and hymns of thanksgiving, she asked the heavenly courtiers to help her in magnifying her most holy son for having thus humiliated Himself in receiving baptism at the hands of one of His creatures.

9. Without delay Christ our Lord pursued His journey from the Jordan to the desert after His baptism. Only His holy angels attended and accompanied Him serving and worshipping Him, singing the divine praises on account of

what He was now about to undertake for the salvation of mankind. He came to the place chosen by Him for His fast, a desert spot among bare and beetling rocks, where there was also a concealed cavern. Here He halted, choosing it for His habitation during the days of His fast. In deepest humility He prostrated Himself upon the ground which was always the prelude of His prayer and that of His most blessed mother. He praised the Eternal Father and gave Him thanks for the works of His divine right hand and for having according to His pleasure afforded Him this retirement. In a suitable manner He thanked even this desert for accepting His presence and keeping Him hidden from the world during the time He was to spend there. He continued His prayers prostrate in the form of a cross, and this was His most frequent occupation in the desert; for in this manner He often prayed to the Eternal Father for the salvation of men. During these prayers, beholding the sins of humanity, and the multitude who would not avail of His sacrifice, He sometimes sweated blood. Although the Lord, as being God, was infinitely above the demon and, as man without deceit of sin, supremely holy and the Master over all creation He nevertheless wished to overcome in His human nature, by His personal justice and holiness, all the vices and their author; and, therefore, He offered His most holy humanity to the buffetings of temptation, concealing His superiority from His invisible enemies.

10. In order to keep informed of the doings of our Saviour the most blessed Mary needed no other assistance than her continual visions and revelations; but in addition to all these, she made use of the service of her holy angels, whom she

sent to her divine son. The Lord Himself thus ordered it, in order that, by means of these faithful messengers, both He and she might rejoice in the sentiments and thoughts of their inmost hearts faithfully rehearsed by these celestial messengers; and thus they each heard the very same words as uttered by each, although both son and mother already knew them in another way. As soon as the great lady understood that our Redeemer was on the way to the desert to fulfil His intention, she locked the doors of her dwelling, without letting anyone know of her presence; and her retirement during the time of our Lord's fast was so complete, that her neighbours thought that she had left with her divine son. She entered into her oratory and remained there for forty days and nights without ever leaving it and without eating anything, just as she knew was done by her most holy son. By His retirement Christ our Lord taught us to conquer the world, the flesh and the devil. All the temptations of the father of lies are accustomed to come cloaked and veiled in deceitful snares. That the Lord should not enter upon His public teaching and make Himself known to the world before He had gained His triumph over the body is another warning and admonition against the weakness of our flesh. He wished to caution us against the honours of this world, even those that accrue to us from supernatural favours, as long as our passions are not conquered and as long as we have not vanquished our common enemies.

GLORY BE TO THE FATHER   Glory be to the Father, and to the Son, and to the Holy Spirit, as it was in the beginning, is now and ever shall be, world without end. Amen.

THE FATIMA PRAYER   O my Jesus, forgive us our sins, save us from the fires of hell, lead all souls to heaven, especially those in most need of Thy mercy.

The Miracle at the Wedding Feast of Cana

THE FRUIT OF THIS MYSTERY

Trust in Our Lady's intercession

 HILE THE QUEEN OF the world was in Cana, her most holy son, with His disciples, was invited to the marriage; and as in His condescension He had brought about this invitation, He accepted it. He betook Himself to this wedding in order to sanctify and confirm the state of matrimony and in order to begin to establish the authenticity of His doctrine by the miracle which He was to perform and of which He was to declare Himself openly as the Author. As He had already proclaimed Himself as the Teacher by admitting His disciples, it was necessary to confirm their calling and give authority to His doctrine in order that they might receive and believe it. Hence, though He had performed other wonders in private, He had not made Himself known as the Author of them in public, as on this occasion.

OUR FATHER   Our Father, Who art in Heaven, hallowed be Thy name, Thy kingdom come, Thy will be done, on earth as it is in heaven. Give us this day our daily bread; and forgive us our trespasses, as we forgive those who trespass against us; and lead us not into temptation, but deliver us from evil. Amen.

HAIL MARY (10)   Hail Mary, Full of Grace, the Lord is with thee. Blessed art thou among women and blessed is the fruit of thy womb, Jesus. Holy Mary, mother of God, pray for us sinners now, and at the hour of our death. Amen.

1. The Blessed lady, being invited to the marriage mentioned by the Evangelist, went to Cana; for it was the marriage of some of her relatives in the fourth degree on her mother's side. While the great Queen was in Cana, the news of the coming of the Redeemer into the world and of His having chosen some disciples had already spread. By the disposition of the Lord, who secretly ordained it for His own high ends, and through the management of His mother, He was called and invited to the wedding with His disciples.

2. The Master of Life entered the house of the marriage feast saluting those present with the words "The peace of the Lord and His light be with you," literally fulfilling them by His arrival. Thereupon He began to exhort and instruct the bridegroom concerning the perfection and holiness of his state of life. In the meanwhile the Queen of heaven instructed the bride in a similar manner, admonishing her in sweetest and yet most powerful words concerning her obligations. Both of the marriage couple afterwards fulfilled most perfectly the duties of their state, into which they were ushered and for which they were strengthened by the sovereigns of heaven and earth.

3. The Lord had not come to this wedding in order to disapprove of matrimony, but in order to establish it anew and give it credit, sanctifying and constituting it a sacrament by His presence. Our Saviour, having exhorted the bridegroom and bride, added a fervent prayer addressed to the Eternal Father, in which He besought Him to pour His blessings upon the institution for the propagation of the human race in the new Law and to vest this state with sacramental power to sanctify all those who would receive it worthily in His holy Church.

4. Our Lord and His most holy mother spoke and conversed with those that came to the wedding; but always with a wisdom and gravity worthy of themselves and with a view of enlightening the hearts of all that were present. The most prudent lady spoke very few words and only when she was asked or when it was very necessary; for she always listened and attended without interruption to the doings

and sayings of the Lord, treasuring them up and meditating upon them in her most pure heart. All the words and behaviour of this great Queen during her life furnish an exquisite example of retirement and modesty; and on this occasion she was an example not only for the religious, but especially for women in the secular state. In women the most precious adornment and the most charming beauty is silence, restraint and modesty by which many vices are shut out and by which all virtues of a chaste and respectable woman receive their crowning grace.

5. At table the Lord and His most holy mother ate some of the food, but with the greatest moderation; yet also without showing outwardly their great abstinence. Although when they were alone they did not eat such food, as I have already recorded, yet these teachers of perfection, who wished not to disapprove of the common life of men, but wished to perfect it, accommodated themselves to all circumstances without any extremes or noticeable singularity wherever it was possible to do so without blame and without imperfection. The Lord not only inculcated this by His example, but He commanded His disciples and apostles to eat of what was placed before them on their evangelical tours of preaching and not to show any singularity in their way of life, such as is indulged in by the imperfect and those little versed in the paths of virtue; for the truly poor and humble must not presume to have a choice in their food.

6. By divine arrangement and in order to give occasion to the miracle, the wine ran out during the meal and the kind lady said to her son, "They have no wine." And the Lord

answered, "Woman, what is that to Me and to you? My hour is not yet come." This answer of Christ was not intended as a reproach, but contained a mystery; for the most prudent Queen had not asked for a miracle by mere accident, but by divine light. She knew that the opportune time for the manifestation of the divine power of her son was at hand. She, who was full of wisdom and knowledge concerning the works of the Redemption and was well informed at what time and on what occasions the Lord was to perform them; therefore, she could not be ignorant of the proper moment for the beginning of this public manifestation of Christ's power. It must also be remembered that Jesus did not pronounce these words with any signs of disapproval, but with a quiet and loving majesty. It is true that He did not address the blessed Virgin by the name of mother, but woman; however, this was because, as I have said before, He had begun to treat her with greater reserve.

7. The mysterious purpose hidden in this answer of Christ was to confirm the disciples in their belief of His Divinity and to show Himself to all as the true God, independent of His mother in His being and in His power of working miracles. On this account, also, He suppressed the tender appellation of mother and called her "woman", saying, "What does it concern you?", or "What part have we, you and I, in this?" As if He wanted to say, "The power of performing miracles I have not received from you, although you have given Me the human nature in which I am to perform them. My Divinity alone is to perform them and for It the hour is not yet come." He wished to give her to understand that the time for working miracles was not to

be determined by His most holy mother, but by the Will of God, even though the most prudent lady should ask for them at an opportune and befitting time. The Lord wished to have it understood that the working of miracles depended upon a higher than the human will, on a will divine and above that of His mother and altogether beyond it; that the will of His mother was to be subject to that which was His as the true God. Hence Christ infused into the minds of the apostles a new light by which they understood the hypostatic union of His two natures, and the derivation of the human nature from His mother and of the divine by generation from His Eternal Father.

8. The blessed lady well understood this mystery and she said with quiet modesty to the servants, "Whatever He says to you, do it." In these words, showing her wise insight into the will of her son, she spoke as the mistress of the whole human race, teaching us mortals, that, in order to supply all our necessities and wants, it was required and sufficient on our part to do all that the Saviour and those taking His place shall command. Such a lesson could not but come from such a mother and advocate, who is so desirous of our welfare and who, since she so well knew what hindrance we place in the way of His great and numerous miracles for our benefits, wishes to instruct us to meet properly the beneficent intentions of the Most High.

9. The Redeemer of the world ordered the servants to fill the jars or water pots, which according to the Hebrew custom had been provided for the occasion. All having been filled, the Lord bade them draw some of the wine into which the

water had been changed, and bring it to the chief steward of the feast, who was at the head of the table and was one of the priests of the Law. When this one had tasted of the wine, he called the bridegroom in surprise and said to him, "Every man at first sets forth good wine, and when men have well drunk, then that which is worse, but you have kept the good wine until now."

10. The steward knew nothing of the miracle when he tasted of the wine; because he sat at the head of the table, while Christ and His mother with His disciples occupied the lower end of the table, practising the doctrine which He was afterwards to teach us; namely, that in being invited to a feast we should not seek to occupy the better places, but be satisfied with the lowest. Then the miracle of changing the water into wine and the dignity of the Redeemer was revealed. The disciples believed anew as the Evangelist says, and their faith in Him was confirmed. Not only them, but many of the others that were present, believed that He was the true Messiah and they followed Him to the City of Capernaum, to where the Evangelist tells us He, with His mother and disciples went from Cana. There, according to saint Matthew, He began to preach, declaring Himself the Teacher of Men.

GLORY BE TO THE FATHER   Glory be to the Father, and to the Son, and to the Holy Spirit, as it was in the beginning, is now and ever shall be, world without end. Amen.

THE FATIMA PRAYER   O my Jesus, forgive us our sins, save us from the fires of hell, lead all souls to heaven, especially those in most need of Thy mercy.

The Proclamation of the Kingdom and the Call to Conversion

 N ALMOST ALL THE miracles and heroic works of Christ, our Redeemer and Master, His most blessed and holy mother concurred and took a part. All that was necessary and sufficient for founding and preserving the Church has been written by the four Evangelists. The many hidden and great works of the exalted Queen have been revealed only to the saints and chosen ones. Even of these revelations, the greater number are better preserved for the beatific vision, where all the blessed shall see these great works manifested to them by the Lord, and where they will eternally praise Him for such magnificent deeds worked through His holy mother.

OUR FATHER   Our Father, Who art in Heaven, hallowed be Thy name, Thy kingdom come, Thy will be done, on earth as it is in heaven. Give us this day our daily bread; and forgive us our trespasses, as we forgive those who trespass against us; and lead us not into temptation, but deliver us from evil. Amen.

HAIL MARY (10)   Hail Mary, Full of Grace, the Lord is with thee. Blessed art thou among women and blessed is the fruit of thy womb, Jesus. Holy Mary, mother of God, pray for us sinners now, and at the hour of our death. Amen.

1. From Cana in Galilee, Christ, the Redeemer, walked to Capernaum, a large and populous city near the sea of Tiberias. Here He remained some days, though not many; for the time of the Pasch was approaching. He gradually drew near to Jerusalem in order to celebrate this feast. His most blessed mother, having rid herself of her house in Nazareth, accompanied Him thenceforth in His tours of preaching and of teaching to the very foot of the cross. She was absent from Him only a few times, as when the Lord absented Himself on Mount Tabor, or on some particular conversions, as for instance that of the Samaritan woman, or when the heavenly lady herself remained behind with certain persons in order to instruct and catechise them.

2. During these journeys the Queen of heaven proceeded on foot, just as her divine son. If even the Lord was fatigued on the way, how much more fatigued was this purest lady? What hardships did she not endure on such arduous journeys in all sorts of weather? Such is the rigorous treatment accorded by the mother of mercy to her most delicate body! What she endured in these labours alone is so great that not all the mortals together can ever satisfy their obligations to her in this regard. Sometimes by permission of the Lord, she suffered such great weakness and pains that He was constrained to relieve her miraculously. At other times He commanded her to rest herself at some stopping place for a few days; while again on certain occasions, He gave such lightness to her body, that she could move about without difficulty as if on wings.

3. The heavenly lady had the whole doctrine of the evangelical law written in her heart. Nevertheless she was as solicitous and attentive as a new disciple to the preaching and doctrine of her divine son, and she had instructed her angels to report to her, if necessary, the sermons of the Master whenever she was absent. To the sermons of her son she always listened on her knees, thus according to the utmost of her powers showing the reverence and worship due to His Person and doctrine. As she was aware at each moment, of the interior operations of the Soul of Christ, and of His continual prayers to the Eternal Father for the proper disposition of the hearts of His hearers and for the growth of the seed of His doctrine into eternal life, the most loving mother joined the Divine Master in His petitions and prayers and in securing for them the blessings of her most

ardent and tearful charity. By her attention and reverence she taught and moved others to appreciate duly the teaching and instructions of the Saviour of the World.

4. Our Lady also knew the interior of those that listened to the preaching of the Lord, their state of grace or sin, their vices and virtues. This various and hidden knowledge, so far above the capacity of men, caused in the heavenly mother many wonderful effects of highest charity and other virtues; it inflamed her with zeal for the honour of the Lord and with ardent desires, that the fruits of the Redemption be not lost to the souls, while at the same time, the danger of their loss to the souls through sin moved her to exert herself in the most fervent prayer for their welfare. She felt in her heart a piercing and cruel sorrow, that God should not be known. adored and served by all His creatures, and this sorrow was in proportion to the unequalled knowledge and understanding she had of all these mysteries. For the souls that would not give entrance to divine grace and virtue she sorrowed with ineffable grief, and used to shed tears of blood at the thought of their misfortune. What the great Queen suffered in this her solicitude and in her labours exceeds beyond all measure the pains endured by all the martyrs of the world.

5. All the followers of the Saviour, and whomever He received into His ministry, she treated with incomparable prudence and wisdom, especially those whom she held in such high veneration and esteem as the apostles of Christ. As a mother she took care of all, and as a powerful Queen she procured necessaries for their bodily nourishment and

comforts. Sometimes, when she had no other resources, she commanded the holy angels to bring provisions for them and for the women in their company. In order to assist them toward advancing in the spiritual life, the great Queen laboured beyond possibility of human understanding; not only by her continual and fervent prayers for them but by her precious example and by her counsels, with which she nourished and strengthened them as a most prudent mother and Teacher. When the apostles or disciples were assailed by any doubts, which frequently happened in the beginning, or when they were attacked by some secret temptation, the great lady immediately hastened to their assistance in order to enlighten and encourage them by the peerless light and charity shining forth in her; and by the sweetness of her words they were exquisitely consoled and rejoiced. They were enlightened by her wisdom, chastened by her humility, quieted by her modesty, enriched by all the blessings that flowed from this storehouse of all the gifts of the Holy Spirit. For all these benefits, for the calling of the disciples, for the conversion and perseverance of the just, and for all the works of grace and virtue, she made a proper return to God, celebrating these events in festive hymns.

6. The innumerable and vast miracles of the great Queen during the public preaching of Christ our Lord are not recorded in the Gospels or in other histories; for the Evangelists spoke only of the wonders performed by Christ and in so far as was useful to establish the faith of the Church. It was necessary that men should first be well established and confirmed in this faith, before the great deeds of the most holy mother should become manifest. According to

what has been given me to understand, it is certain that she brought about not only many miraculous conversions, but she cured the blind and the sick, and called the dead to life. That this should be so was proper for many reasons, on the one hand, she was the assistant in the principal work for which the Incarnate Word came into the world, namely in His preaching and His Redemption; for thereby the Eternal Father opened up the treasures of His Omnipotence and infinite Goodness, manifesting them in the Divine Word and in the heavenly mother. On the other hand, she as His mother was to resemble her son in the working of miracles, increasing the glory of both; for in this way she accredited the dignity and doctrine of her son and eminently and most efficaciously assisted Him in His ministry. That these miracles should remain concealed, was due both to the disposition of divine Providence and to the earnest request of Mary herself; hence she performed them with such a wise secrecy, that all the glory redounded to the exaltation of the Redeemer in whose name and virtue they were carried out.

7. By conversation and familiar encounters with their great Queen and lady the reverential love and devotion of the disciples and apostles both grew and increased. As the great lady, on account of her peerless insight knew the natural disposition of each of the disciples, his measure of grace, his present condition and future office, she proceeded according to this knowledge in her petitions and prayers, in her instructions and conversations with them, and in the favours she obtained for each in support of his vocation. Such a loving zeal in the conduct of a mere creature excited a new and boundless admiration in the holy angels. Of no less

admiration was the hidden providence of the Almighty by which the apostles were made to correspond to the blessings and favours received by them at the intercession of the most holy mother. All this caused a divine harmony of action, hidden to men and manifest only to the heavenly spirits.

8. Our Saviour continued to perform His miracles in Judea. Among them was also the resurrection of Lazarus in Bethany, to where He had been called by the two sisters, Martha and Mary. As this miracle took place so near to Jerusalem, the report of it was soon spread throughout the city. Six days after the miracle Our Lord again visited Bethany and was there entertained by the two sisters. They had arranged a banquet for the Lord and His mother, and for all of His company. Among those that were at table with them, was also Lazarus, whom he had brought back to life a few days before. The priests and Pharisees, being irritated by this miracle, held a council in which they resolved upon the death of the Redeemer and commanded all those that had any knowledge of His whereabouts to make it known.

9. While our Saviour, according to the custom of the Jews, was reclining at this banquet, Magdalen, filled with divine enlightening and most magnanimous sentiments, entered the banquet hall. As an outward token of her ardent love toward Christ, her Divine Master, she anointed His feet and poured out over them and over His head an alabaster vase filled with a most fragrant and precious liquor, composed of spikenard and other aromatic ingredients. Then she wiped His feet with her hair just as she had done at another occasion in the house of the Pharisee, related by saint Luke.

Although the other three Evangelists apparently differ as to some of the circumstances; yet I was informed that each anointing was certainly done by Magdalen, who was moved to these acts of devotion by inspiration of the Holy Spirit and by her own burning love toward Christ the Redeemer. The fragrance of this ointment filled the whole house, for she had procured a large quantity, and of the most precious kind; nor did she stint it in any way, but broke the vessel in token of her generous love and devotion to the Master.

10. Magdalen also had a share in Our Lady's special love; for the Blessed mother knew that the love of this woman for her son was most ardent and that this great penitent was eminently chosen for the manifestation of the magnificence of God's mercy toward men. Most holy Mary distinguished her before the other women in her familiar company and enlightened her in regard to most exalted mysteries, by which she inflamed still more the love of Magdalen toward Jesus and toward herself. The holy penitent consulted the heavenly lady in regard to her desire of retreating into solitude in order to live in continual contemplation and penance; and the sweetest mother instructed her in the deep mysteries of solitary life. This life she afterwards embraced with the consent and blessing of the Queen. Later on Mary visited her in her retreat in person and by means of the angels often encouraged and consoled Magdalen in the horrors of the desert. The other women, who were in the company of Jesus, were much favoured by the most blessed mother; all of them and all the disciples of the Lord experienced her incomparable kindness and they were filled with an intense devotion and affection toward the mistress and

mother of grace. They drew of the treasures of grace from her as from a storehouse, where God had laid up His gifts for the whole human race.

GLORY BE TO THE FATHER   Glory be to the Father, and to the Son, and to the Holy Spirit, as it was in the beginning, is now and ever shall be, world without end. Amen.

THE FATIMA PRAYER   O my Jesus, forgive us our sins, save us from the fires of hell, lead all souls to heaven, especially those in most need of Thy mercy.

The Transfiguration of the Lord on Mount Tabor

To enter the cloud of unknowing and perceive the presence of God

URING OUR LORD'S TRANSFIGURATION, the blessed Mary, who was mystically present, saw not only the humanity of Christ our Lord transformed in glory, but she was favoured by an intuitive and clear vision of the Divinity Itself; for the Lord wished her to partake of the privilege implied in being present at this event in a more abundant and distinguished manner than the apostles. Moreover, there was a great difference between her insight and that of the apostles into the glory of the transfigured body; for the apostles, as saint Luke tells us, were not only asleep when Jesus at the beginning of this mysterious glorification retired to pray, but they were also seized with such fear at the voice resounding from heaven, that they fell with their faces to the earth and rose not until the Lord Himself spoke to them and raised them up. The Blessed Mother, on the other hand, witnessed and heard all these events without undue excitement; for, besides being accustomed to such great manifestations of glory, she was divinely fortified and enlightened for looking upon the Divinity. Hence she was enabled to look fixedly upon the glorified body, without experiencing the terror and weakness of the senses which overtook the apostles.

OUR FATHER   Our Father, Who art in Heaven, hallowed be Thy name, Thy kingdom come, Thy will be done, on earth as it is in heaven. Give us this day our daily bread; and forgive us our trespasses, as we forgive those who trespass against us; and lead us not into temptation, but deliver us from evil. Amen.

HAIL MARY (10)   Hail Mary, Full of Grace, the Lord is with thee. Blessed art thou among women and blessed is the fruit of thy womb, Jesus. Holy Mary, mother of God, pray for us sinners now, and at the hour of our death. Amen.

1. Our Redeemer and Master Jesus had already consumed more than two years and a half in preaching and performing

wonders, and He was approaching the time predestined by the eternal wisdom for satisfying divine justice, for redeeming the human race through His passion and death and thus to return to His Eternal Father. Since all His works were ordered with the highest wisdom for our instruction and salvation, the Lord resolved to prepare and strengthen some of His apostles for the scandal of His passion by manifesting to them beforehand in its glory that same body, which He was so soon to exhibit in the disfigurement of the cross. Thus would they be reassured by the thought, that they had seen it transfigured in glory before they looked upon it disfigured by His sufferings. This He had promised a short time before in the presence of all, although not to all, but only to some of His disciples.

2. For His Transfiguration Our Lord selected a high mountain in the centre of Galilee, two leagues east of Nazareth and called Mount Tabor. Ascending to its highest summit with the three apostles, Peter, and the two brothers James and John, He was transfigured before them. The three Evangelists tell us that besides these apostles, were present also the two prophets, Moses and Elijah, discoursing with Jesus about His passion, and that, while He was thus transfigured, a voice resounded from heaven in the name of the Eternal Father, saying, "This is My beloved Son, in Whom I am well pleased, listen to Him."

3. The countenance of Our Lord's holy face began to shine like the sun and His garments became whiter than the snow. This outward splendour was merely the effect of the glory of His Divinity always united to His beatified soul.

At His Incarnation, the glory which would naturally have been communicated permanently to His sacred body was miraculously suspended for the time of His natural life. Now, this suspension of His divine glory ceased, and the body, for a short time, was allowed to share the glory of His soul. This is the splendour which became visible to those who were present. Immediately after the miraculous suspense, the divine glory was again confined only to His soul. As His soul was always in the beatified state, so also His body, according to the common order, should have continually shared in this glory, and therefore this transient glorification of His body was likewise a miracle.

4. The Evangelists do not say that most holy Mary was present at this Transfiguration, nor do they say that she was not there; this did not fall within their purpose, and they did not think it proper to speak of the hidden miracle by which she was enabled to be there. For the purpose of recording this event here, I was given to understand that at the same time in which some of the holy angels were commissioned to bring the soul of Moses and Elijah from their abode, others of her own guard carried the heavenly lady to Mount Tabor, in order to witness the Transfiguration of her divine son, for without a doubt she really witnessed it.

5. There was no necessity of confirming the most holy mother in her faith, as was necessary with the apostles; for she was invincibly confirmed in faith. But the Lord had many different objects in view at His Transfiguration; and there were special reasons for His not wishing to celebrate this great event without the presence of His most

holy mother. What for the apostles was a gratuitous favour, was a duty in regard to the Queen and mother, since she was His Companion and Co-partner in the works of the Redemption even to the foot of the cross. It was proper to fortify her by this favour against the torments in store for her most holy soul.

6. Our Lady was to remain on earth as the teacher of the holy Church, therefore it was proper that she should also be one of the eyewitnesses of this great mystery. To grant such a favour was easily within the power of her divine son, since He was accustomed to lay open to her all the workings of His divine soul. Nor would the love of such a son permit Him to withhold that favour from His mother; for He otherwise omitted nothing whereby He could in any way demonstrate His tender love for her, and this certainly would be a token of highest esteem for her excellence and dignity. I have, therefore, been informed that for these reasons and for many others not necessary to mention here, most holy Mary assisted at the Transfiguration of her divine son, our Redeemer.

7. The Blessed Mother had already on other occasions seen the body of her divine son glorified, but on this occasion, she looked upon Him with much greater enlightenment and with a mind much more alert to all the wonders therein hidden. Hence, also, the effects caused in her by this vision were such that she was totally renewed and inflamed by this communication with the Divinity. As long as she lived she never lost the impression caused by the sight of such glory manifested in the humanity of Christ. The memory

of it greatly consoled her in the absence of her divine son and whenever His glorious presence was not otherwise felt by her. Yet on the other hand the memory of this glorious Transfiguration of Christ also made her feel so much the more deeply the maltreatment experienced by Christ in His passion and death.

8. No human ingenuity can suffice fully to describe the effects of this glorious vision of her son on her most holy soul. With inmost gratitude and deepest penetration she began to ponder upon what she had seen and heard; exalted praise of the omnipotent God welled forth from her lips, when she considered how her eyes had seen refulgent in glory that same bodily substance, which had been formed of her blood, carried in her womb and nursed at her breast; how she had with her own ears heard the voice of the Eternal Father acknowledge her son as His own and appoint Him as the Teacher of all the human race. With her holy angels she composed new canticles to celebrate an event so full of festive joy for her soul and for the most sacred humanity of her son.

9. After the Transfiguration the most Blessed Mother was brought back to her house in Nazareth; her divine son descended the mountain and immediately came to visit her in order to take final leave of His parental province and set out for Jerusalem. There, on the following Pasch, which was to be for Him the last upon earth, He was to enter upon His passion.

10. Having spent only a few days at Nazareth, He departed with His mother, His disciples and apostles and some of the holy women, travelling about through Galilee and Samaria before entering Judea and Jerusalem. He set His face toward Jerusalem; for He journeyed to Jerusalem with a joyous countenance and full of desire to enter upon His sufferings, in order thereby, according to His own most ardent and generous desire, to sacrifice Himself for the human race. He was not to return to Galilee, where He had performed so many miracles. Knowing this at His departure from Nazareth, He glorified His Eternal Father and, in the name of His sacred humanity, gave thanks for having, in that house and neighbourhood, received the human form and existence which He was now to deliver over to suffering and death.

GLORY BE TO THE FATHER   Glory be to the Father, and to the Son, and to the Holy Spirit, as it was in the beginning, is now and ever shall be, world without end. Amen.

THE FATIMA PRAYER   O my Jesus, forgive us our sins, save us from the fires of hell, lead all souls to heaven, especially those in most need of Thy mercy.

The Institution of the Holy Eucharist

THE FRUIT OF THIS MYSTERY

Tears for the profanations of the Most Holy Sacrament, the true Body of Christ

OMENTS BEFORE THE CONSECRATION of the Blessed Sacrament, all those present were overtaken with a profound sense of wonder at what the Author of Life intended to do. There appeared in the hall the person of the Eternal Father and of the Holy Spirit as they had appeared at the baptism of Christ at the Jordan and at the Transfiguration on mount Tabor. Although all the apostles and disciples felt this divine presence, yet only some of them really were favoured with a vision of it; among these was especially saint John the Evangelist, who was always gifted with eagle sight into the divine mysteries. The entire heaven was transplanted to the Cenacle of Jerusalem; for of such great importance was the magnificence of this work, by which the new Church was founded, the law of grace established and eternal salvation made secure. The great lady, from her retreat, beheld in divine contemplation all these doings of her son in the Cenacle; and in her profound intelligence she entered more deeply into their meaning than the apostles and the angels, who also were present in bodily forms, adoring their true Lord, Creator and King. By the hands of these angels Enoch and Elijah were brought to the Cenacle from their place of abode; for the Lord wished that these Fathers of the natural and of the written Laws should be present at the establishment of the law of the Gospel, and that they should participate in its mysteries.

OUR FATHER   Our Father, Who art in Heaven, hallowed be Thy name, Thy kingdom come, Thy will be done, on earth as it is in heaven. Give us this day our daily bread; and forgive us our trespasses, as we forgive those who trespass against us; and lead us not into temptation, but deliver us from evil. Amen.

HAIL MARY (10)   Hail Mary, Full of Grace, the Lord is with thee. Blessed art thou among women and blessed is

the fruit of thy womb, Jesus. Holy Mary, mother of God, pray for us sinners now, and at the hour of our death. Amen.

1. Thursday, the eve of the passion and death of the Saviour, had arrived; at earliest dawn the Lord called His most beloved mother and she, hastening to prostrate herself at His feet, responded; "Speak, my Lord and Master, for your servant is listening." Raising her up from the ground, He spoke to her in words of soothing and tenderest love, "My mother, the hour decreed by the eternal wisdom of My Father for accomplishing the salvation and restoration of the human race and imposed upon Me by His most holy and acceptable will, has now arrived; it is proper that now we subject to Him our own will, as we have so often offered to do. Give Me your permission to enter upon My suffering and death, and, as My true mother, consent that I deliver Myself over to My enemies in obedience to My Eternal Father. Of your own free will, you didst consent to My Incarnation, so I now desire you to give consent also to My passion and death of the cross." These words of the Saviour, spoken on that occasion, pierced the most loving heart of Mary and cast her into the throes of a sorrow greater than she had ever endured before. She remembered the obedience He had shown her as His mother during so many years and the blessings He had conferred upon her during His long association with her; she realised that soon she was to be deprived of this blessed company and of the beauty of His countenance, of the vivifying sweetness of His words; that she was not only to lose all this at once, but moreover that she was to deliver Him over into the hands of such wicked enemies, to ignominies and torments and to the

bloody sacrifice of a death on the cross. How deeply must all these considerations and circumstances, now so clearly before her mind, have penetrated into her tender and loving heart and filled it with a sorrow unmeasurable! But with the magnanimity of a Queen, vanquishing this invincible pain, she prostrated herself at the feet of her divine son and Master, and, in deepest reverence, kissing His feet, answered, "Lord and highest God, Author of all that has being, though You are the son of my womb, I am Your handmaid; I offer myself and resign myself to the divine pleasure of The Father, in order that in Me, just as in You, my son and Lord, His eternal and adorable will may be fulfilled."

2. The apostles asked Him where He wished to celebrate the paschal supper; for on that Thursday night the Jews were to partake of the lamb of the Pasch, a most notable and solemn national feast. This eating of the paschal lamb was the most prophetic and significant feast of the Jews in anticipation of the Messiah and of the mysteries connected with Him and His work. Even so, the apostles were as yet scarcely aware of its intimate connection with Christ. The Divine Master answered by sending saint Peter and saint John to Jerusalem to make arrangements for the paschal lamb. This was to be in a house where they would see a servant enter with a jug of water, and whose master they were to request in Christ's name to prepare a room for His last supper with His disciples. This man lived near to Jerusalem; rich and influential, he was at the same time devoted to the Saviour and was one of those who had witnessed and had believed in His miracles and teachings. The Author of Life rewarded his piety and devotion by choosing his house for

the celebration of the great mystery, and thus consecrate it as a temple for the faithful of future times. The two apostles immediately departed on their commission and following the instructions, they asked the owner of this house to entertain the Master of Life for the solemn celebration of this feast of the unleavened bread.

3. The heart of this householder was enlightened by special grace and he readily offered his dwelling with all the necessary furniture for celebrating the supper according to the law. He assigned to them a very large hall, appropriate tapestries and adorned for the mysteries which, unbeknown to him and the apostles, the Lord was to celebrate therein. After due preparation had thus been made the Saviour and the other apostles arrived at this apartment. His most blessed mother and the holy women in her company came soon after. Upon entering, the most humble Queen prostrated herself on the floor and adored her divine son as usual, asking His blessing and begging Him to let her know what she was to do. He bade her go to another room, where she would be able to see all that was done on this night according to the decrees of providence, and where she was to console and instruct, as far as was proper, the holy women of her company. The great lady obeyed and retired with her companions. She exhorted them to persevere in faith and prayer, while she, knowing that the hour of her Holy Communion was at hand, continued to keep her interior vision riveted on the doings of her most holy son and to prepare herself for the worthy reception of His body and blood.

4. His most holy mother having retired, our Lord and Master, Jesus, with His apostles and disciples, took their places to celebrate the feast of the lamb. He observed all the ceremonies of the Law, as prescribed by Himself through Moses. During this last supper He gave to the apostles an understanding of all the ceremonies of the figurative law, as observed by the Patriarchs and Prophets. He showed them how beneath it was hidden the real truth, namely, all that He Himself was to accomplish as Redeemer of the world. He made them understand, that now the law of Moses and its figurative meaning was evacuated by its real fulfilment. He told them that, by celebrating this supper, He set an end to the rites and obligations of the old Law, which was only a preparation and a representation of what He was now about to accomplish, and hence having attained its end, had now become useless. This instruction enlightened the apostles concerning the deep mysteries of this last supper. The other disciples that were present did not understand these mysteries as thoroughly as the apostles. Judas attended to and understood them least of all, indeed, not at all; for he was completely under the spell of his avarice, thinking only of his prearranged treason and how he could execute it most secretly.

5. Having completed the supper and fully instructed His disciples, Christ our Saviour, as saint John tells us, arose from the table in order to wash their feet. He first prostrated Himself before His Eternal Father and addressed to Him, "Eternal Father, Creator of the universe, In order to leave an example of humility to My apostles and to My Church, which must be built up on the secure foundation of this

virtue, I desire, My Father, to wash the feet of My disciples, including the least of all of them, who is My enemy." The Master arose from His prayer and, His countenance beaming with peace and serenity, commanded His disciples to seat themselves like persons of superior station, while He Himself remained standing as if He were their servant. Then He laid aside the mantle, which He wore over the seamless garment and which covered all His Person except the feet. He girded His body with one end of a large towel, permitting the other part to hang down free. Then He poured water into a basin for washing the feet of the apostles, who were wonderingly observing the proceedings of their Divine Master.

6. Having washed the feet of Peter, the Divine Master then proceeded to wash also the feet of Judas, whose perfidious treason could not prevent the charity of Christ from secretly bestowing upon him tokens of even greater charity than upon the other apostles. Without permitting it to be noticed by the others, He manifested His special love toward Judas in two ways. On the one hand, in the kind and caressing manner in which He approached him, knelt at his feet, washed them, kissed them and pressed them to His bosom. On the other hand, by seeking to move his soul with inspirations proportionate to the dire depravity of his conscience; for the assistance offered to Judas was in itself much greater than that offered to the other apostles. But as the disposition of this apostle was most wicked, his vices deeply ingrown upon him, his understanding and his faculties much disturbed and weakened; as he had entirely forsaken God and given himself over to the devil, and, as he had enthroned the evil spirit in his heart; he resisted all

the divine advances and inspirations connected with this washing of his feet. He was moreover harassed by the fear of breaking his contract with the scribes and Pharisees. As the bodily presence of Christ and the interior urgency of His inspirations both stormed his sense of right, there arose within his darkened soul a dreadful hurricane of conflicting thoughts, filling him with dismay and bitterness, and fiercest anger, whirling him still farther away from his Saviour and turning the divine balsam applied to his soul into deadly poison of hellish malice and total depravity. Thus it came that the malice of Judas resisted the saving contact of those divine hands, in which the Eternal Father had placed miraculous power to enrich all creatures with His blessings.

7. The Lord seated Himself at this table with the apostles and some of the other disciples, and then ordered some unleavened bread to be placed on the table and some wine to be brought, of which He took sufficient to prepare the chalice. Thereupon Christ our Lord took into His venerable hands the bread, which lay upon the plate, and interiorly asked the permission and cooperation of the Eternal Father, that now and ever afterwards in virtue of the words about to be uttered by Him, and later to be repeated in His holy Church, He should really and truly become present in the host, Himself to yield obedience to these sacred words. While making this petition He raised His eyes toward heaven with an expression of such sublime majesty that He inspired the apostles, the angels and His Virgin Mother with new and deepest reverence. Then He pronounced the words of consecration over the bread, changing its substance into the substance of His true body and immediately thereupon

He·uttered the words of consecration also over the wine, changing it into His true blood. As an answer to these words of consecration was heard the voice of the Eternal Father, saying, "This is My beloved Son, in Whom I delight, and shall take My delight to the end of the world" In like manner was this confirmed by the Holy Spirit. The most sacred humanity of Christ, in the Person of the Word, gave tokens of profoundest veneration to the Divinity contained in the Sacrament of His body and blood. The Virgin Mother, in her retreat, prostrated herself on the ground and adored her son in the Blessed Sacrament with incomparable reverence. Then also the angels of her guard, all the angels of heaven, and among them likewise the souls of Enoch and Elijah, in their own name and in the name of the holy Patriarchs and Prophets of the old law, fell down in adoration of their Lord in the holy Sacrament.

8. All the apostles and disciples, who, with the exception of the traitor, believed in this holy Sacrament, adored it with great humility and reverence according to each one's disposition. The great high priest Christ raised up His own consecrated body and blood in order that all who were present at this first Mass might adore it in a special manner, as they also did. During this elevation His most pure mother, saint John, Enoch and Elijah, were favoured with an especial insight into the mystery of His presence in the sacred species. They understood more profoundly, how, in the species of the bread, was contained His body and in those of the wine, His blood; how in both, on account of the inseparable union of His soul with His body and blood, was present the living and true Christ; how with the Person

of the Word, was also therein united the Person of the Father and of the Holy Spirit; and how therefore, on account of the inseparable existence and union of the Father, Son and Holy Spirit, the holy Eucharist contained the perfect humanity of the Lord with the three divine Persons of the Godhead. All this was understood most profoundly by the heavenly lady and by the others according to their degree. They understood also the efficacy of the words of the consecration, now endowed with such divine virtue, that as soon as they are pronounced with the intention of doing what Christ did at that time, by any priest since that time over the proper material, they would change the bread into His body and the wine into His blood, leaving the accidents to subsist in a new way and without their proper subject. They saw, that this change would take place so certainly and infallibly, that heaven and earth would sooner fall to pieces, than that the effect of these words of consecration, when pronounced in the proper manner by the sacerdotal minister of Christ, should ever fail.

9. While receiving His own body and blood Christ our Lord composed a canticle of praise to the Eternal Father and offered Himself in the blessed Sacrament as a sacrifice for the salvation of man. He took another particle of the consecrated bread and handed it to the Archangel Gabriel who brought and communicated it to the most holy Mary. By having such a privilege conferred on one of their number, the holy angels considered themselves sufficiently recompensed for being excluded from the sacerdotal dignity and for yielding it to man. The privilege of merely having even one of their number hold the sacramental body of their

Lord and true God filled them with a new and immense joy. In abundant tears of consolation the great Queen awaited Holy Communion. When saint Gabriel with innumerable other angels approached, she received it, the first after her son, imitating His self-abasement, reverence and holy fear. The most blessed Sacrament was deposited in the breast and above the heart of the most holy Virgin Mother, as in the most legitimate shrine and tabernacle of the Most High. There the ineffable sacrament of the holy Eucharist remained deposited from that hour until after the Resurrection, when saint Peter said the first Mass and consecrated anew. After having thus favoured the heavenly princess, our Saviour distributed the sacramental bread to the apostles, commanding them to divide it among themselves and partake of it. By this commandment He conferred upon them the sacerdotal dignity and they began to exercise it by giving Communion each to himself. This they did with the greatest reverence, shedding copious tears and adoring the body and blood of our Lord, Whom they were receiving. They were established in the power of the priesthood, as being founders of the holy Church and enjoying the distinction of priority over all others.

10. The perfidious and treacherous Judas, hearing the command of his Master to partake of Holy Communion, resolved in his unbelief not to comply, but if he could do so without being observed, determined to secrete the sacred body and bring it to the priests and Pharisees in order to afford them a chance of incriminating Jesus by showing them what He had called His own body; or if he should not succeed therein, to consummate some other vile act of

malice with the divine Sacrament. The mistress and Queen of heaven, who by a clear vision was observing all that passed and knew the interior and exterior effects and affections in the apostles at Holy Communion, saw also the accursed intentions of the obstinate Judas. All the zeal for the glory of her Lord, existing in her as His mother, spouse and Daughter, was aroused in her purest heart. Knowing that it was the divine will, that she should make use of her power as mother and Queen, she commanded the holy angels to extract from the mouth of Judas the consecrated particles as well of the bread as of the wine and replace them from whence they had been taken. It well befitted her on this occasion to defend the honour of her divine son and prevent Judas from heaping such an ignominious injury upon Christ the Lord. The holy angels obeyed their Queen, and when it was the turn of Judas to communicate, they withdrew the consecrated species one after the other, and, purifying them from their contact with Judas, the most wicked of living men, they restored them to their place, altogether unobserved by the disciples. Thus the Lord shielded the honour of His malicious and obstinate apostle to the end. This was attended to by the angels in the shortest space of time and the others then received Holy Communion, for Judas was neither the first nor the last to communicate. Then our Saviour offered thanks to the Eternal Father and therewith ended both the legal and the sacramental supper in order to begin the mysteries of His passion.

GLORY BE TO THE FATHER   Glory be to the Father, and to the Son, and to the Holy Spirit, as it was in the beginning, is now and ever shall be, world without end. Amen.

THE FATIMA PRAYER   O my Jesus, forgive us our sins, save us from the fires of hell, lead all souls to heaven, especially those in most need of Thy mercy.

CONCLUDING PRAYERS   *Upon completing the recitation of the Holy Rosary, the following prayers are customary, but others too may be added according to one's devotion and preference.*

HAIL HOLY QUEEN   Hail Holy Queen, mother of Mercy, hail our life, our sweetness and our hope. To thee do we cry, poor banished children of Eve, to thee do we send up our sighs, mourning and weeping in this vale of tears. Turn then, most gracious advocate, thine eyes of mercy towards us, and after this, our exile, show unto us the blessed fruit of thy womb, Jesus. O clement, O loving, O sweet Virgin Mary. Pray for us O holy mother of God, that we may be made worthy of the promises of Christ.

Let Us Pray   O God, Whose only begotten son, by His life, death and resurrection, has purchased for us the rewards of eternal life, grant we beseech Thee, that meditating on these mysteries of the most Holy Rosary of the Blessed Virgin Mary, we may both imitate what they contain and obtain what they promise, through the same Christ our Lord. Amen.

PRAYER TO SAINT MICHAEL THE ARCHANGEL   Holy Michael, Archangel, defend us in the day of battle. Be our safeguard against the wickedness and snares of the devil. May God rebuke him, we humbly pray; and do thou, O Prince of the heavenly hosts, by the power of God thrust down

into hell Satan and all the evil spirits who wander through the world seeking the ruin of souls. Amen.

MEMORARE   Remember, O most gracious Virgin Mary, that never was it known that anyone who fled to thy protection, implored thy help, or sought thine intercession was left unaided. Inspired by this confidence, I fly unto thee, O Virgin of virgins, my mother; to thee do I come, before you I stand, sinful and sorrowful. O mother of the Word Incarnate, despise not my petitions, but in thy mercy hear and answer me. Amen.

May the Divine Assistance remain always with us, and may the souls of the faithful departed, through the mercy of God rest in peace. Amen.

The Hopeful Mysteries

The Creation of all things in Christ

FRUIT OF THIS MYSTERY

Wonder at Our Lady Immaculate, as predestined from the beginning

N THE BEGINNING, EVEN before the foreknowledge
of sin, according to our way of understanding, the
promise and, as it were, the decree, was made by
the Word as to the degree of sanctity, and perfection and
the gifts and graces, which were to be possessed by Mary
His mother. Also as to the protection, support and defence,
which was to be provided for this true City of God, in which

His Majesty contemplated the graces and merits, which she earned for herself, as well as the fruits to be gathered for His people by the loving returns, which she was to make to His Majesty. In the same instant, God determined to create a locality and an abode, where the Incarnate Word and His mother should converse and dwell. For them primarily did He create the heaven and earth with its stars and elements and all that is contained in them.

OUR FATHER   Our Father, Who art in Heaven, hallowed be Thy name, Thy kingdom come, Thy will be done, on earth as it is in heaven. Give us this day our daily bread; and forgive us our trespasses, as we forgive those who trespass against us; and lead us not into temptation, but deliver us from evil. Amen.

HAIL MARY (10)   Hail Mary, Full of Grace, the Lord is with thee. Blessed art thou among women and blessed is the fruit of thy womb, Jesus. Holy Mary, mother of God, pray for us sinners now, and at the hour of our death. Amen.

1. O King, most high and most wise Lord, How incomprehensible are Your judgments, and inscrutable Your ways! Invincible God, enduring forever and whose beginning is unknown! Who can understand Your greatness and who can be worthy of Your most magnificent works, or who can tell You why You have created them? For You are exalted above all of them and our vision cannot reach You and our understanding cannot comprehend You. May You be blessed, magnificent King, because You have deigned to show me, Your slave and a vile worm of the earth, great wonders and

most sublime mysteries, exalting my habitation and raising my spirit to a height, in which I saw things unspeakable. I saw the Lord and Creator of all things; I perceived as it were the exaltedness of a Being existing in Itself, before It created any other thing; I do not know the manner in which He showed Himself to me, but I know, truly, what I saw and perceived.

2. I saw the Most High, at the same time understanding how His Majesty is in Himself; I received a clear intelligence and a true perception of what is meant by a God, infinite in His substance and attributes, eternal, exalted above all, being three in Person, and one true God. Three in Person, because of the three activities of knowing, comprehending and loving each other; one, so as to secure the boon of eternal unity. It is the Trinity of the Father, the Son and the Holy Spirit. I saw the Lord as He was before He had created anything and with great astonishment I looked to see where was the throne of the Most High, for the empyrean heavens were not, nor the lower ones, nor did the sun exist, nor the moon, nor the other stars, nor the elements, only the Creator was, without any of His creatures. All was void, without presence of angels, or men or animals. I saw how of necessity it must be admitted, that God has His being in Himself, and that He stands in want or need of none of the created things.

3. When God resolved upon the creation of the whole world, in that instant, the Son was not only coexistent in divine essence with the Father and the Holy Spirit, but also the human nature, which He was to assume, was foreseen and

conceived as the prototype of all works in the divine mind
of the Father. Conjointly with Him was also foreseen as
present the human nature of His most holy mother, who
was to conceive Him in her most pure womb. In these two
Persons were foreseen all His works, so that on account
of Them He overlooked all that could offend Him in the
conduct of the men and angels that were to fall.

4. I understood the Incarnation of the Divine Word necessarily to have been the first incentive and object on account
of which, before all others, the divine intelligence and will
created anything; and the reasons are most exalted, so that
I cannot explain. One of these reasons is, that God, having
in Himself known and loved Himself, should, according to
right order, know and love that, which approaches most inti-
mately to His Divinity, as is the case in the hypostatic union.
Another reason is, that the Divinity, having communicated
Itself ad intra, should also communicate Itself ad extra, for
thus the divine will and intention would begin to execute
Its works with the highest end in view, and His attributes
would be communicated in the most beautiful order.

5. To this instant also, and, as it were, in natural sequence,
pertain the decree and predestination of the mother of the
Divine Word Incarnate; for here, I understand, was ordained
that pure creature before anything else at all. Thus, before
all other creatures, was she conceived in the divine mind,
in such manner and such state as befitted and became the
dignity, excellence and gifts of the humanity of her most
holy son. To her flowed over, at once and immediately, the
river of the Divinity and its attributes with all its impetuosity,

in as far as a mere creature is capable and as is due to the dignity of the Mother of God.

6. The Most High looked upon His Son and upon His most holy mother as models, produced in the culmination of His wisdom and power, in order that They might serve as prototypes according to which He was to copy the whole human race. Thus the rest of men depended on these two as mediators between themselves and God. He created also the necessary material beings required for human life, but with such wisdom, that some of them also serve as symbols, to represent in a certain way these two beings, which He primarily intended and to which all others were to be subservient, namely, Christ and most holy Mary.

7. On this account of Jesus and Mary, Almighty God made the luminaries of heaven, the sun and the moon, so that in dividing the day and the night, they might symbolise the Sun of justice, Christ, and His most holy mother, who is beautiful as the moon. These two divide the day of grace and the night of sin. The sun illuminates the moon; and both, together with the stars of the firmament, illumine all other creatures within the confines of the universe. He created the rest of the beings and added to their perfection, because they were to be subservient to Christ and most holy Mary, and through them to the rest of men.

8. In the knowledge of these exalted mysteries and decrees, I confess myself ravished in admiration and transported beyond my proper self. Perceiving this most holy and pure creature formed and conceived in the divine mind from the

beginning and before all the ages, I joyously and exultingly magnify the Omnipotent for the admirable and mysterious decree, by which He formed for us such a pure and grand, such a mysterious and godlike creature, worthy rather to be admired and praised by all beings, than to be described by anyone. In my admiration I can say with St. Dionysus the Areopagite, "If faith would not instruct me, and if the understanding of what I see would not teach me, that it is God, who has conceived her in His mind, and who alone could and can in His Omnipotence form such an image of His Divinity, I might begin to doubt, whether the Virgin Mother herself were not, in fact, divine."

9. O what tears flowed from my eyes, and what sorrowful astonishment possessed my soul, to see that divine prodigy not acknowledged and that wonder of the Most High not manifest to all the mortals. Much is known of it, but much more is unknown, as this sealed book has not been opened. I am ravished in the perception of this tabernacle of God, and I perceive that the Author of it is more admirable in her creation, than in that of all the rest of the world, although the diversity of the creatures manifests the wonderful power of their Creator. In this Queen alone are comprehended and contained more treasures than in all the rest of things joined together, and the variety and the preciousness of her riches honour the Lord above all the multitudes of the other creatures.

10. Lastly was decreed the creation of a people and congregation of men for Christ, who was already formed in the divine mind and will, and according to whose image and

likeness man was to be made, in order, that the Incarnate Word might find brethren, similar but inferior to Himself and a people of His own nature, of whom He might be the Head. In this instant was determined the order of the creation of the whole human race, which was to begin from one man and woman and propagate itself, until the Virgin and her son should be born in the predestined order. On account of the merits of Christ, our Saviour, the graces and gifts were prearranged, and also original justice, if they would only preserve it. The fall of Adam was then foreseen and in him that of all others, except of the Queen, who did not enter into this decree, being separate in predestination with her son. All that was convenient and necessary for the conservation of the human race and for obtaining the end of the Redemption and the Predestination, was then preordained, without interfering with the free will of men; for such ordainment was more conformable to God's nature and to divine equity.

GLORY BE TO THE FATHER   Glory be to the Father, and to the Son, and to the Holy Spirit, as it was in the beginning, is now and ever shall be, world without end. Amen.

THE FATIMA PRAYER   O my Jesus, forgive us our sins, save us from the fires of hell, lead all souls to heaven, especially those in most need of Thy mercy.

The Promise of the Redeemer and Co-Redemptrix

THE FRUIT OF THIS MYSTERY
Resolution for frequent sacramental Confession

HEN LUCIFER SAW THE two fallen and their interior beauty and grace and original justice changed into the ugliness of sin, he celebrated his triumph with incredible joy and vaunting in the company of his demons. But he soon fell from his proud boasting, when he saw, contrary to his expectations, how kindly the merciful love of

God dealt with the delinquents, and how He offered them a chance of doing penance by giving them hope of pardon and return of grace. Moreover he saw how they were disposing themselves toward this forgiveness by sorrow and contrition, and how the beauty of grace was restored to them. When the demons perceived the effect of contrition, all hell was again in confusion. His consternation grew, when he heard the sentence, which God pronounced against the guilty ones, in which he himself was implicated. More especially and above all was he tormented by the repetition of that threat, "The woman shall crush your head", which he had already heard in heaven.

OUR FATHER   Our Father, Who art in Heaven, hallowed be Thy name, Thy kingdom come, Thy will be done, on earth as it is in heaven. Give us this day our daily bread; and forgive us our trespasses, as we forgive those who trespass against us; and lead us not into temptation, but deliver us from evil. Amen.

HAIL MARY (10)   Hail Mary, Full of Grace, the Lord is with thee. Blessed art thou among women and blessed is the fruit of thy womb, Jesus. Holy Mary, mother of God, pray for us sinners now, and at the hour of our death. Amen.

1. On the sixth day Almighty God formed and created Adam, as it were of the age of thirty-three years. This was the age in which Christ was to suffer death, and Adam in regard to his body was so like unto Christ, that scarcely any difference existed. Also according to the soul Adam was similar to Christ. From Adam God formed Eve so similar

to the Blessed Virgin, that she was like unto her in personal appearance and in figure.

2. But the happy state in which God had created the parents of the human race lasted only a very short while. The envy of the serpent was immediately aroused against them, for Satan was impatiently awaiting their creation, and no sooner were they created, than his hatred became active against them. However, he was not permitted to witness the formation of Adam and Eve, as he had witnessed the creation of all other things, for the Lord did not choose to manifest to him the creation of man, nor the formation of Eve from a rib; all these things were concealed from him for a space of time. God looked upon Adam and Eve with the highest pleasure and benevolence, and on account of them as the first parents He heaped many blessings upon them, as if He wanted to entertain Himself with them and their descendants until the time should arrive for forming Christ and Mary.

3. Lucifer, from the beginning, laboured under ignorance concerning the mystery and the time of the Incarnation, and a mystery surrounding the formation of Adam and Eve. The Evil One suspected that Adam had come forth from Eve, and that she was the mother and Adam the Incarnate Word. His suspicions grew, when he felt the divine power, which prevented him from harming the life of these creatures. On the other hand he soon became aware of the commandments that God gave them, for these he had heard pronounced. Being freed more and more from his doubt as he listened to the words of the first parents and sized up their natural

gifts, he began to follow them like a roaring lion, seeking an entrance through those inclinations, which he found in each of them. Nevertheless he continued to hesitate between his wrath against Christ and Mary and the dread of being overcome by Them. Most of all he dreaded the confusion of being conquered by the Queen of heaven, who was to be a mere creature and not God.

4. Lucifer entered with all his energy upon the work of entrapping them and of opposing and hindering the execution of the Divine Will. He first approached the woman, and not the man, because he knew her to be by nature more frail and weak, and because in tempting her he would be more certain that it was not Christ whom he was encountering. Against her also he was more enraged ever since God had shown him the prophetic sign in the heaven that he would be conquered by a woman. His wrath was greater against Eve than against Adam.

5. Before Lucifer showed himself to Eve, he aroused in her many disturbing thoughts or imaginations, in order to approach her in a state of excitement and pre-occupation. He took the form of a serpent, and thus speaking to Eve drew her into a conversation, which she should not have permitted. Listening to him and answering, she began to believe him; then she violated the command of God, and finally persuaded her husband likewise to transgress the precept. Thus, ruin overtook them and all the rest, for themselves and for us they lost the happy position, in which God had placed them.

6. The offspring of Eve multiplied after the fall and so arose the distinction and the multiplication of the good and the bad, the elect and the reprobate, the ones following Christ the Redeemer, and the others following Satan. The elect cling to their Leader by faith, humility, charity, patience and all the virtues and in order to obtain victory, they are assisted, helped and beautified by the divine grace and the gifts, which the Redeemer and Lord of all merited for them. But the reprobate, without receiving any such benefits from their false leader, or earning any other reward than the eternal pain and the confusion of hell, follow him in pride, presumption, obscenity and wickedness, being led into these disorders by the father of lies and the originator of sin.

7. As the world progressed in its course, in order that the Word might descend from the bosom of the Father and clothe Itself in our mortality, God selected and prepared a chosen and most noble people, the most admirable of past and future times. Within it also He constituted a most illustrious and holy race, from which He was to descend according to the flesh. He reared most holy Prophets and Patriarchs, who in figures and prophecies announced to us from far off, that, which we have now in possession. To this people God manifested His Immutable Essence by many revelations, and they again transmitted these revelations to us by the Holy Scriptures, containing immense mysteries, which we grasp and learn to know by faith. All of them, however, are brought to perfection and are made certain by the Incarnate Word, who transmitted to us the secure rule of faith and the nourishment of the sacred Scriptures in His Church.

8. Although the Prophets and the just ones of that people were not so far favoured as to see Christ in His body, they nevertheless experienced the liberality of the Lord, who manifested Himself to them by prophecies and who moved their hearts to pray for His coming and for the Redemption of the whole human race. The consonance and harmony of all these prophecies, mysteries and aspirations of the ancient fathers, were a sweet music to the Most High, which resounded in the secret recesses of the Divinity and which regaled and shortened the time, to speak in a human manner, until He should descend to converse with man.

9. But who can worthily exalt the benefits Almighty God provided for His people in the praiseworthy host of holy Prophets, through whom the Lord has spread the light of prophecy, lighting up as from afar the holy Church, and commencing in advance to shed the rays of the Sun of Justice and of the efficacious law of grace. The two great Prophets, Isaiah and Jeremiah, were chosen to preach to us, in a sweet and exalted manner, the mysteries of the Incarnation of the Word, His Birth, Life and Death. Wonder and suspense fill me in the consideration of these prophets. God wished all His great works to be announced, prophesied and prefigured far in advance and so completely, that they might testify the love and care, which He had for men and with which He enriched His Church. He wished also to reprehend us and convict us of our lukewarmness, since these ancient Fathers and Prophets, seeing only the shadows and figures, were inflamed with divine love and broke forth in canticles of praise and exaltation of the Lord, whereas we, who enjoy the truth and the bright day of grace, remain buried in

forgetfulness of so great benefits, and, forsaking the light, continue to seek the darkness.

10. The posterity and race of Adam spread out in great numbers, for the just and the unjust were multiplied; likewise did increase the clamours of the just for the Redeemer, and the transgressions of the wicked in demerit of that benefit. The people of the Most High and the plans for the triumph of the Lord in assuming human nature, were already in the last stages of preparation for the advent of the Messiah. The kingdom of sin in the generation of the wicked had now spread its dominion to the utmost limits and the opportune time for the remedy had arrived. The merits and the crowns of the just had been multiplied, the Prophets and the holy Fathers in the joy of heavenly enlightenment perceived the approach of the salvation and the presence of the Redeemer, and they increased their clamours, beseeching God to fulfil the prophecies and the promises made to His people. Before the high throne of the divine mercy they asked God to remember the diffuse and sombre night of sin which had lasted since the creation of the first man, and the blindness of idolatry, which had taken hold of all the rest of the human race.

GLORY BE TO THE FATHER   Glory be to the Father, and to the Son, and to the Holy Spirit, as it was in the beginning, is now and ever shall be, world without end. Amen.

THE FATIMA PRAYER   O my Jesus, forgive us our sins, save us from the fires of hell, lead all souls to heaven, especially those in most need of Thy mercy.

The Birth of the Immaculate Virgin Mary to Sts. Joachim and Ann

THE FRUIT OF THIS MYSTERY

Honour of father and mother

HE HOLY ARCHANGEL GABRIEL appeared to saint Ann in human form more resplendent than the sun, and said to her, "Ann, servant of God, I am an angel sent from the council of the Most High, who in divine condescension looks upon the humble of the earth. Good is incessant prayer and humble confidence. The Lord has heard your petitions, for He is near to those who call upon Him with living faith and hope, and who expect His salvation. If He delays hearing their clamours and defers the fulfilment of their prayers, it is in order to dispose them to receive and to oblige Himself to give much more than they ask and desire. You and Joachim have prayed for the Fruit of benediction and the Most High has resolved to give you holy and wonderful Fruit. The humility, faith and the alms of Joachim and of yourself have come before the throne of the Most High and now He sends me, His angel, in order to give you news full of joy for your heart, His Majesty wishes, that you be most fortunate and blessed. He chooses you to be the mother of her who is to conceive and bring forth the Only Begotten of the Father. You shall bring forth a Daughter, who by divine disposition shall be called Mary. She shall be blessed among women and full of the Holy Spirit. She shall be the cloud that shall drop the dew of heaven for the refreshment of mortals, and in her shall be fulfilled the prophecies of your ancestors. She shall be the portal of life and salvation for the sons of Adam. Know also that I have announced to Joachim, that he shall have a daughter who shall be blessed and fortunate, but the full knowledge of the mystery is not given him by the Lord, for he does not know, that she is to be the mother of the Messiah. Therefore you must guard this secret; and go now to the temple to give thanks to the Most High for having been so highly favoured by His powerful right hand. In the Golden Gate you shall meet Joachim, where you will confer with him about this tiding. You are the one who is especially blessed of the Lord and to whom He wishes to visit and enrich with more singular blessings. In solitude

He will speak to your heart and there give a beginning to the law of grace, since in your womb He will give being to her, who is to vest the Immortal with mortal flesh and human form. In this humanity, united with the Word, will be written, as with His own blood, the true law of Mercy,"

OUR FATHER   Our Father, Who art in Heaven, hallowed be Thy name, Thy kingdom come, Thy will be done, on earth as it is in heaven. Give us this day our daily bread; and forgive us our trespasses, as we forgive those who trespass against us; and lead us not into temptation, but deliver us from evil. Amen.

HAIL MARY (10)   Hail Mary, Full of Grace, the Lord is with thee. Blessed art thou among women and blessed is the fruit of thy womb, Jesus. Holy Mary, mother of God, pray for us sinners now, and at the hour of our death. Amen.

1. After many years, the ancient serpent had infected the whole earth with his poisonous breath and apparently enjoyed peaceful control over mortals who had become blind to the light of reason, and to the precepts contained in the ancient testament given to Israel. At this Juncture, the Most High directed His attention to the attribute of His mercy, to the clamours of the just and the prayers of the prophets of His chosen people. The Almighty resolved to give most certain pledges of the day of grace, sending into the world two most bright luminaries to announce the approaching dawn of the sun of Justice, Christ our Salvation. These were saint Joachim and Ann, prepared and created by especial decree according to His own heart.

2. Saint Joachim had his home, his family and relations in Nazareth, a town of Galilee. He, always a just and holy man and illumined by especial grace and light from on high, had a knowledge of many mysteries of the Holy Scriptures and of the ancient prophets. In continual and fervent prayer he asked of God the fulfilment of His promises, and his faith and charity penetrated the heavens. He was a man most humble and pure, leading a most holy and sincere life, yet he was most grave and earnest, and incomparably modest and honest.

3. The most fortunate Ann had a house in Bethlehem and was a most chaste, humble and beautiful maiden. From her childhood she led a most virtuous, holy and retired life, enjoying great and continual enlightenment in exalted contemplation. Nevertheless, she was most diligent and industrious, thus attaining perfection in both the active and the contemplative life. She had an infused knowledge of the Divine Scriptures and a profound understanding of its hidden mysteries and wonders. In the infused virtues of faith, hope and love she was unexcelled. Equipped with all these gifts, she continued to pray for the coming of the Messiah. Her prayers were so acceptable to the Lord, that to her He could but answer with the words of the spouse, "You have wounded My heart with one of the hairs of your neck." Therefore, without doubt, saint Ann holds a high position among the saints of the Old Testament, who by their merits hastened the coming of the Redeemer.

4. The two holy spouses lived in Nazareth, continuing to walk in the justification of the Lord. In rectitude and

sincerity they practised all virtue in their works, making themselves very acceptable and pleasing to the Most High and avoiding all blemish in all their doings. They themselves lived with each other in undisturbed peace and union of heart, without quarrel or shadow of a grudge. The most humble Ann subjected herself and conformed herself in all things to the will of Joachim, and that man of God, with equal emulation of humility, sought to know the desires of holy Ann, confiding in her with his whole heart, and he was not deceived. Thus they lived together in such perfect charity, that during their whole life they never experienced a time, during which one ceased to seek the same thing as the other. This fortunate couple passed twenty years of their married life without issue. In those times and among the people of the Jews this was held to be the greatest misfortune and disgrace. On this account they had to bear much reproach and insult from their neighbours and acquaintances, for all those that were childless, were considered as excluded from the benefits of the Messiah. But the Most High wished to afflict them and dispose them for the grace which awaited them, in order that in patience and submission they might tearfully sow the glorious fruit, which they were afterwards to bring forth. They continued in most fervent prayers from the bottom of their hearts, mindful of the command from on high. They made an express vow to the Lord, that if He should give them issue, they would consecrate It to His service in the temple of Jerusalem.

5. Having, at the command of the Lord, persevered a whole year in fervent petitions, it happened by divine inspiration and ordainment, that Joachim was in the temple of Jerusalem

offering prayers and sacrifices for the coming of the Messiah, and for the fruit, which he desired. Arriving with others of his town to offer the common gifts and contributions in the presence of the high priest, Issachar, an inferior priest, harshly reprehended the old and venerable Joachim, for presuming to come with the other people to make his offerings in spite of his being childless. He, a holy man, full of shame and confusion, in humble love thus addressed the Lord, "Most high Lord and God, at Your command and desire I came to the temple; he that takes Your place, despises me; my sins merit this disgrace; but since I accept it according to Your will, do not cast away the creature of Your hands" Joachim hastened away from the temple full of sorrow, though peaceful and contented, to a farm or storehouse, which he possessed, and there in solitude he called upon the Lord for some days.

6. While Joachim was making petitions in his retirement, the holy angel manifested to holy Ann, that her prayer for a child, accompanied by such holy desires and intentions, was pleasing to the Almighty. Having thus recognised the will of God and of her husband Joachim, she prayed with humble subjection and confidence, that it be fulfilled. The petitions of the holy Joachim and Ann reached the throne of the Holy Trinity, where they were accepted and the will of God was made known to the holy angels. The three divine Persons, according to our way of expressing such things, interiorly reflected as follows, "We have in our condescension resolved, that the Person of the Word shall assume human flesh and that through Him all the race of mortals shall find a remedy. We have already manifested and promised

this to our servants, the Prophets, in order that they might announce it to the world. The sins of the living, and their malice are so great, that We are much constrained by the rigour of justice. But our goodness and mercy is greater than all their evil-doing, nor can it extinguish Our love toward men. We will look with mercy upon the works of our hands, which We have created according to our image and likeness, so as to enable them to become inheritors and participators of our eternal glory. We will consider the services and the pleasure derived from Our servants and friends and regard the multitude of those, who shall distinguish themselves in Our praise and friendship. And above all have We before our eyes her, who is to be the chosen one, who is to be acceptable above all creatures and singled out for Our delight and pleasure; because she is to conceive the person of the Word in her womb and clothe Him with human flesh. Since there must be a beginning of this work, by which We shall manifest to the world the treasures of the Divinity, this shall be the acceptable and opportune time for its execution. Joachim and Ann have found grace in our eyes; We look upon them with pleasure and shall enrich them with choicest gifts and graces. They have been faithful and constant in their trials and in simplicity and uprightness their souls have become acceptable and pleasing before Us. Let Gabriel as Our ambassador bring tidings of joy for them and for the whole human race; let him announce to them, that in Our condescension We have looked upon them and chosen them."

7. Thus the celestial spirits were instructed in regard to the will and the decree of the Almighty. The holy Archangel

Gabriel humbled himself before the throne of the most Blessed Trinity, adoring and revering the divine Majesty in the manner which befits these most pure and spiritual substances. From the throne an intellectual voice proceeded, saying, "Gabriel, enlighten, vivify and console Joachim and Ann, our servants, and tell them, that their prayers have come to our presence and their petitions are heard in clemency. Promise them, that by the favour of our right hand they will receive the Fruit of benediction, and that Ann shall conceive a Daughter, to whom We give the name of Mary." Together with this mandate of the Most High many mysteries and wonders pertaining to this message were revealed to saint Gabriel. With it he descended from the vault of the empyrean heaven and appeared to holy Joachim, while he was in prayer, saying "Just and upright man, the Almighty from His sovereign throne has taken notice of your desires and has heard your sighs and prayers, and has made you fortunate on earth. Your spouse Ann shall conceive and bear a daughter, who shall be blessed among women. The nations shall know her as The Blessed. He who is the eternal God, uncreated, and the Creator of all, most upright in His judgments, powerful and strong, sends me to you, because Your works and alms have been acceptable. Love has softened the heart of the Almighty, and has hastened His mercies, and in His liberality He wishes to enrich your house and your family with a daughter, whom Ann shall conceive; the Lord Himself has chosen for her the name of Mary. From her childhood let her be consecrated to the temple, and in it to God. She shall be elect, exalted, powerful and full of the Holy Spirit; on account of the sterility of Ann her conception shall be miraculous; she shall be a daughter wonderful in all her doings and in all her life. Praise the Lord, Joachim, for this benefit and magnify Him, for in no other nation has He done anything like this. You shall go to give thanks in the temple of Jerusalem and in testimony of the truth of this joyful message, you shall meet, in the Golden Gate, your beloved Ann, who is coming to the temple for the same purpose. Remember that marvellous is this message, for the Conception of this child shall rejoice heaven and earth."

8. In the meanwhile the thrice blessed Ann was in prayer and divine contemplation, totally wrapped up in the mystery of the Incarnation, which she humbly solicited from the Eternal Word. Saint Ann had received an enlightenment regarding this ineffable mystery and she continually reflected upon it. She dwelt upon all the words which she had learned from her guardian angel, who on many occasions, and now more openly than ever before, had manifested Himself to her. The Almighty ordained that the message of the Conception of His holy mother should, in some way, be similar to the one by which the Incarnation would be announced. Indeed, saint Ann was meditating in humble fervour upon her, who was to bear the Mother of the Incarnate Word, just as the most holy Virgin would later make the same reflections upon her, who was to be the Mother of God. It was also the same angel that brought both messages, and in human form, though he showed himself in a more beautiful and mysterious shape to the Virgin Mary.

9. Immediately arising from contemplation, and the message of Holy Gabriel, St. Ann hastened to the temple of

Jerusalem, and there found saint Joachim, as the angel had foretold to them both. Together they gave thanks to the Almighty for this wonderful blessing and offered special gifts and sacrifices. They were enlightened anew by the grace of the Holy Spirit, and, full of divine consolation, they returned to their home. Joyfully they conversed about the favours, which they had received from the Almighty, especially concerning each one's message of the Archangel Gabriel, whereby, on behalf of the Lord, they had been promised a daughter who should be most blessed and fortunate. On this occasion they also told each other, how the same angel, before their espousal, had commanded each to accept the other, in order that together they might serve God according to His divine will. This secret they had kept from each other for twenty years, without communicating it, until the same angel had promised them the issue of such a daughter. Anew they made the vow to offer her to the temple and that each year on this day they would come to the temple to offer special gifts, spend the day in praise and thanksgiving, and give many alms. This vow they fulfilled to the end of their lives, spending this day in great praise and exaltation of the Most High. The prudent matron Ann never disclosed the secret, that her daughter was to be the mother of the Messiah, either to Joachim or to any other creature. Nor did that holy parent Joachim, in the course of his life, know any more than that she was to be a grand and mysterious woman. However, in the last moments of his life the Almighty made the secret known to him.

10. The day destined for the birth of her, who was consecrated and sanctified to be the Mother of God, had arrived,

a day most fortunate for the world. This birth happened on the eighth day of September, fully nine months having elapsed since the Conception of the soul of our most holy Queen and lady. Saint Ann was prepared by an interior voice of the Lord, informing her, that the hour of her parturition had come. Full of the joy of the Holy Spirit at this information, she prostrated herself before the Lord and besought the assistance of His grace and His protection for a happy deliverance. Presently she felt a movement in her womb similar to that which is proper to creatures being born to the light. The most blessed child Mary was at the same time by divine providence and power ravished into a most high ecstasy. Hence Mary was born into the world without perceiving it by her senses, for their operations and faculties were held in suspense. As she had the use of her reason, she would have perceived it by her senses, if they would have been left to operate in their natural manner at that time. However, the Almighty disposed otherwise, in order that the princess of heaven might be spared the sensible experience otherwise connected with birth. She was born pure and stainless, beautiful and full of grace, thereby demonstrating, that she was free from the law and the tribute of sin. Although she was born substantially like other daughters of Adam, yet her birth was accompanied by such circumstances and conditions of grace, that it was the most wonderful and miraculous birth in all creation and will eternally redound to the praise of her Maker. At twelve o'clock in the night this holy child issued forth, dividing the night of the ancient Law and its pristine darknesses from the new day of grace, which now was about to break into dawn. She was clothed, handled and dressed like other infants, though her soul dwelt near to the Divinity; and she was treated as an infant, though she excelled all mortals and even all the angels in wisdom. Her mother did not allow her to be touched by other hands than her own, but she herself wrapped her in swaddling clothes, and in this Saint Ann was not hindered by her present state of childbirth; for she was free from the toils and labours, which other mothers usually endure in such circumstances. So then saint Ann received in her arms her who was her daughter, but, at the same time, the most exquisite treasure of all the universe, inferior only to God and superior to all other creatures. With fervent tears of joy she offered praise to His Majesty.

GLORY BE TO THE FATHER   Glory be to the Father, and to the Son, and to the Holy Spirit, as it was in the beginning, is now and ever shall be, world without end. Amen.

THE FATIMA PRAYER   O my Jesus, forgive us our sins, save us from the fires of hell, lead all souls to heaven, especially those in most need of Thy mercy.

The Presentation of Mary, as a Girl, in the Temple

THE FRUIT OF THIS MYSTERY

Desire to spend greater time before the Blessed Sacrament

N THE ANCIENT ARK of the Covenant Mary was foreshadowed as the great Queen, who was to be the depositary of all that God provided and operated for His creatures. As the Ark, Mary also enclosed within herself the manna of the Divinity and of grace, and the wonder-working staff of miracles and prodigies. This heavenly and mystical Ark alone contained the fountain of grace, namely God Himself, overflowing into the rest of mankind and forming the nucleus of all the miracles and prodigies of God. In Mary, therefore, all that the Lord desired to operate and manifest is contained and deposited. Such a sacred and mysterious Ark, constructed by the hands of the Lord Himself for His habitation and as the propitiatory of His people, could not remain with propriety outside of His temple, where the material ark had been preserved, which, indeed, was only a figure of this spiritual and true Ark of the new covenant. Therefore its Author ordained that she be placed in His house and temple as soon as the first three years of her infancy should be completed.

OUR FATHER   Our Father, Who art in Heaven, hallowed be Thy name, Thy kingdom come, Thy will be done, on earth as it is in heaven. Give us this day our daily bread; and forgive us our trespasses, as we forgive those who trespass against us; and lead us not into temptation, but deliver us from evil. Amen.

HAIL MARY (10)   Hail Mary, Full of Grace, the Lord is with thee. Blessed art thou among women and blessed is the fruit of thy womb, Jesus. Holy Mary, mother of God, pray for us sinners now, and at the hour of our death. Amen.

1. After her purification Saint Ann renewed the vow, which she had already made, to offer her firstborn to the temple on arriving at the proper age. In renewing this offering she was enlightened by new graces and promptings of the Most High, and in her heart she heard a secret voice urging her to fulfil this vow and offer her child to the temple within

three years. It was as it were the echo of the voice of the most holy Queen, who in her prayer touched the heart of God, in order that it might resound in the bosom of the mother. For when both entered the temple, the sweet child seeing with her bodily eyes its grandeur and magnificence, dedicated to the worship and adoration of the Divinity, experienced wonderful effects of the Spirit and wished to prostrate herself in the temple, to kiss its floor, and adore the Lord. But as she could not execute these desires in external actions, she supplied the defect with interior fervour, and she adored and blessed the Lord with a love more ardent, and a humility more profound than ever before or ever after was possible to be rendered by any creature.

2. The sovereign child, Mary, was treated like other children of her age. Her nourishment was of the usual kind, though less in quantity; and so was her sleep, although her parents were solicitous that she take more sleep. She was not troublesome, nor did she ever cry for mere annoyance, as is done by other children, but she was most amiable and caused no trouble to anybody. That she did not act in this regard as other children caused no wonder; for she often wept and sighed (as far as her age and her dignity of Queen and mistress would permit) for the sins of the world and for its Redemption through the coming of the Saviour. Ordinarily she maintained, even in her infancy, a pleasant countenance, yet mixed with gravity and a peculiar Majesty, never showing any childishness. She sometimes permitted herself to be caressed, though, by a secret influence and a certain outward austerity, she knew how to repress the imperfections connected with such endearments. Her prudent

mother Ann treated her child with incomparable solicitude
and caressing tenderness; also her father Joachim loved her
as a father and as a saint, although he was ignorant of the
mystery at that time. The child on its part showed a special
love toward him, as one whom she knew for her father
and one much beloved of God. Although she permitted
more tender caresses from her father than from others, yet
God inspired the father as well as all others, with such an
extraordinary reverence and modesty towards her whom he
had chosen for his mother, that even his pure and fatherly
affection was outwardly manifested only with the greatest
moderation and reserve.

3. In all things the infant Queen was most gracious, perfect
and admirable. Though she passed her infancy subject to the
common laws of nature, yet this did not hinder the influx
of grace. During her sleep her interior acts of love, and all
other exercises of her faculties which were not dependent
on the exterior senses, were never interrupted. This special
privilege is possible also in other creatures, if the divine
power confers it on them; but it is certain that in regard to
her whom He had chosen as His mother and the Queen
of all creation, He extended this special favour beyond all
previous or subsequent measure in other creatures and
beyond the conception of any created mind. God spoke
to Samuel and to other saints and Prophets in their sleep,
and to many He sent mysterious dreams or visions for to
His Omnipotence it is easy to enlighten the mind during
the inactivity of the senses in natural sleep or during their
ravishment in ecstasy; they cease to act in the one as well
as in the other, and without their activity the soul hears,

accepts and transacts the things of the Spirit. This was the rule which the Queen followed from the moment of her conception till now and for all eternity; for the activity of grace in her during her pilgrimage through life was not intermittent, like in other creatures. When she was alone, or when she was laid to sleep, which was in her most moderate, she was engaged in the contemplation of the mysteries and the excellencies of the Most High, and in the enjoyment of the divine visions and the conversation of His Majesty.

4. The family of Joachim was not rich, though at the same time he could not have been called poor. Conformable to the honoured standing of her family, saint Ann desired to dress her most holy daughter as best she could afford within the bounds of decency and modesty. The most humble child yielded to this maternal solicitude during the time of her voluntary silence without protest; but when she began to speak, she humbly asked her mother not to clothe her in costly and showy garments, but to procure for her garments of coarse and poor material, if possible, such as had already been worn by others and of an ash-grey colour, similar to that which in our day is worn by the nuns of saint Clare. The holy mother, who looked upon and respected her daughter as her mistress, answered, "My daughter, I will conform to your desire in regard to the form and colour of your dress; but your strength will not permit the coarseness which you desires, and in this regard I wish that you obey me." The child obedient to the will of her mother and never objecting in anything, acquiesced and allowed herself to be clothed in the garments which were provided. They were of the colour and form desired by her, and similar to the dress

worn by children dedicated to a devout life. Although she desired them to be coarser and poorer, she supplied this want by obedience, deeming obedience more precious than sacrifice. Thus the most holy child Mary had the merit of obedience to her mother and of humility in her aspirations, deeming herself unworthy of the use of even that which is necessary to preserve natural life. In the virtue of obedience toward her parents she was most distinguished and exact during the three years of her stay with them; by her divinely infused science she knew their interior wishes and thus she was beforehand in fulfilling them to the minutest point. She asked the permission and blessing of her mother for whatever she undertook to do herself, kissing her hand with great humility and reverence. The mother outwardly permitted this, while inwardly she venerated the grace and exalted dignity of her daughter.

5. A few days before most holy Mary reached the age of three years, she was favoured with an abstract vision of the Divinity, in which it was made known to her that the time of her departure for the temple ordained by God, had arrived, and that there she was to live dedicated and consecrated to His service. Her most pure soul was filled with new joy and gratitude at this prospect. At that time saint Ann also had a vision, in which the Lord enjoined her to fulfil her promise by presenting her daughter in the temple on the very day, on which the third year of her age should be complete. There is no doubt that this command caused more grief in saint Ann, than that given to Abraham to sacrifice his son Isaac. But the Lord consoled and comforted her, promising His grace and assistance in her loneliness during the

absence of her beloved daughter. The holy matron showed herself prepared and ready to execute the command of the Almighty, and she answered full of submission to Almighty God. Saint Joachim also had a visitation or vision of the Lord at this time, receiving the same command as Ann. Having conferred with each other and taking account of the will of the Lord, they resolved to fulfil it with humble submission and appointed the day on which the child was to be brought to the temple. Great was also the grief of this holy old man, though not quite so great as that of saint Ann, for the high mystery of her being the future Mother of God was yet concealed from him.

6. The three years decreed by the Lord having been completed, Joachim and Ann set out from Nazareth, accompanied by a few of their kindred and bringing with them the true living Ark of the covenant, the most holy Mary, borne on the arms of her mother in order to be deposited in the holy temple of Jerusalem. The beautiful child, by her fervent and loving aspirations, hastened after the ointments of her Beloved, seeking in the temple Him, whom she bore in her heart. This humble procession was scarcely noticed by earthly creatures, but it was invisibly accompanied by the angelic spirits, who, in order to celebrate this event, had hastened from heaven in greater numbers than ordinary as her bodyguard, and were singing in heavenly strains the glory and praise of the Most High. The princess of heaven heard and saw them as she hastened her beautiful steps along in the sight of the highest and the true Solomon. Thus they pursued their journey from Nazareth to the holy city of

Jerusalem, and also the parents of the holy child Mary felt in their hearts great joy and consolation of spirit.

7. They arrived at the holy temple, and the blessed Ann on entering took her daughter and mistress by the hand, accompanied and assisted by saint Joachim. All three offered a devout and fervent prayer to the Lord; the parents offering to God their daughter, and the most holy child, in profound humility, adoration and worship, offering up herself. She alone perceived that the Most High received and accepted her, and, amid divine splendour which filled the temple, she heard a voice saying to her, "Come, My Beloved, My spouse, come to My temple, where I wish to hear your voice of praise and worship." Having offered their prayers, they rose and betook themselves to the priest. The parents consigned their child into his hands and he gave them his blessing. Together they conducted her to the portion of the temple buildings, where many young girls lived to be brought up in retirement and in virtuous habits, until old enough to assume the state of matrimony. It was a place of retirement especially selected for the first-born daughters of the royal tribe of Judah and the sacerdotal tribe of Levi.

8. Fifteen stairs led up to the entrance of these apartments. Other priests came down these stairs in order to welcome the blessed child Mary. The one that had received them, being according to the law one of a minor order, placed her on the first step. Mary, with his permission, turned and kneeling down before Joachim and Ann, asked their blessing and kissed their hands, recommending herself to their prayers before God. The holy parents in tenderest tears

gave her their blessing; whereupon she ascended the fifteen stairs without any assistance. She hastened upward with incomparable fervour and joy, neither turning back, nor shedding tears, nor showing any childish regret at parting from her parents. To see her, in so tender an age, so full of strange majesty and firmness of mind, excited the admiration of all those present. The priests received her among the rest of the maidens, and saint Simeon consigned her to the teachers, one of whom was the prophetess Anna. This holy matron had been prepared by the Lord by especial grace and enlightenment, so that she joyfully took charge of this child of Joachim and Ann. She considered the charge a special favour of Divine Providence and merited by her holiness and virtue to have her as a disciple, who was to be the Mother of God and mistress of all the creatures.

9. Sorrowfully her parents Joachim and Ann retraced their journey to Nazareth, now poor as deprived of the rich treasure of their house. But the Most High consoled and comforted them in their affliction. The holy priest Simeon, although he did not at this time know of the mystery enshrined in the child Mary, obtained great light as to her sanctity and her special selection by the Lord; also the other priests looked upon her with great reverence and esteem. In ascending the fifteen stairs the child brought to fulfilment, that, which Jacob saw happening in sleep; for here too were angels ascending and descending, the ones accompanying, the others meeting their Queen as she hastened up; whereas at the top God was waiting in order to welcome her as His daughter and spouse. She also felt by the effects of the

overflowing love, that this truly was the house of God and the portal of heaven.

10. The child Mary, when brought to her teacher, knelt in profound humility before her and asked her blessing. She begged to be admitted among those under her direction, obedience and counsel, and asked her kind forbearance in the labour and trouble which she would occasion. The prophetess Anna, her teacher, received her with pleasure, and said to her, "My daughter, you shall find in me a helpful mother and I will take care of you and of your education with all possible solicitude." Then the holy child proceeded to address herself with the same humility to all the maidens which were then present; each one she greeted and embraced, offering herself as their servant and requesting them, as older and more advanced than she in the duties of their position, to instruct and command her. She also gave them thanks that, without any merit in their sight, they admitted her to their company.

GLORY BE TO THE FATHER   Glory be to the Father, and to the Son, and to the Holy Spirit, as it was in the beginning, is now and ever shall be, world without end. Amen.

THE FATIMA PRAYER   O my Jesus, forgive us our sins, save us from the fires of hell, lead all souls to heaven, especially those in most need of Thy mercy.

The Chaste Espousals of Mary and Joseph

THE FRUIT OF THIS MYSTERY

Admiration of St. Joseph, Our Lady's spouse most chaste

 N THE DAY ON which our princess Mary completed the fourteenth year of her life, the men,
who at that time in the city of Jerusalem were
descendants of the tribe of Judah and of the race of David,
gathered together in the temple. The sovereign lady was also

of that lineage. Among the number was Joseph, a native of Nazareth, and then living in Jerusalem; for he was one of the descendants of the royal race of David. He was then thirty-three years of age, of handsome person and pleasing countenance, but also of incomparable modesty and gravity; above all he was most chaste in thought and conduct, and most saintly in all his inclinations. From his twelfth year he had made and kept the vow of chastity. He was related to the Virgin Mary in the third degree, and was known for the utmost purity of his life, holy and irreprehensible in the eyes of God and of men.

OUR FATHER   Our Father, Who art in Heaven, hallowed be Thy name, Thy kingdom come, Thy will be done, on earth as it is in heaven. Give us this day our daily bread; and forgive us our trespasses, as we forgive those who trespass against us; and lead us not into temptation, but deliver us from evil. Amen.

HAIL MARY (10)   Hail Mary, Full of Grace, the Lord is with thee. Blessed art thou among women and blessed is the fruit of thy womb, Jesus. Holy Mary, mother of God, pray for us sinners now, and at the hour of our death. Amen.

1. At the age of thirteen and a half years, having grown considerably for her age, our most charming princess, most pure Mary, had another abstractive vision of the Divinity of the same order and kind as those already described. In this vision, we might say, happened something similar to that which the Holy Scriptures relate of Abraham, when God commanded him to sacrifice his beloved son Isaac, the only

pledge of all his hopes. God tempted Abraham, says Moses, trying and probing the promptness of his obedience in order to reward it. We can say the same thing of our great lady, that God tried her in this vision, by commanding her to enter the state of matrimony. Thence we can also understand the truth of the words, "How inscrutable are the judgments of the Lord and how exalted are His ways and thoughts above our own!" As distant as heaven is from earth, were the thoughts of most holy Mary from the plans which the Most High now made known to her, by commanding her to accept a husband for her protection and company; for as far as depended upon her will she had desired and resolved during all her life not to have a husband and she had often repeated and renewed the vow of chastity, which she had taken at such a premature age.

2. The Lord had celebrated His solemn espousal with the princess Mary when she was brought to the temple, confirming and approving her vow of chastity, and solemnising it by the presence of the glorious hosts of angels. The most innocent dove had withdrawn herself from all human interactions, relinquishing entirely all that might be called worldly interest and attention, or love and desire of creatures. She was altogether taken up and transformed by the pure and chaste love of that highest Good which never fails, knowing that she would be only more chaste in its love, more pure in its contact, and more virginal in its acceptance. When therefore, without any other explanation, the command of the Lord reached her, that she now accept an earthly spouse and husband, what surprise and astonishment was it to this heavenly maid, who, in her fixed confidence was living so

secure in the possession of God Himself as her spouse and who now heard from Him such a command? Greater was this trial than that of Abraham, for he did not love Isaac in the same degree as most holy Mary loved inviolate chastity. Nevertheless at this unexpected command the most prudent Virgin suspended her judgment, and preserved the calmness of her hope and belief more perfectly than Abraham. After many days of prayer and entreaty, the Lord appeared to her and said to her, "My spouse and my dove, let your afflicted heart expand and let it not be disturbed or sad; I will attend to your yearnings and to your requests, I will direct all things, and will govern the priests by my enlightenment; I will give you a spouse selected by Myself, and one who will put no hindrance to your holy desires, but who, by my grace will prosper you in them. I will find for you a perfect man conformable to my heart and I will choose him from the number of My servants; My power is infinite, and My protection and aid shall never fail you."

3. While our great lady continued to apply herself to vigilant prayer, God spoke in sleep to the high priest, saint Simeon, and commanded him to arrange for the marriage of Mary, the daughter of Joachim and Ann of Nazareth; since he regarded her with special care and love. The holy priest answered, asking what was His will in regard to the person, whom the maiden Mary was to marry and to whom she was to give herself as spouse. The Lord instructed him to call together the other priests and learned persons and to tell them that this maiden was left alone and an orphan and that she did not desire to be married; but that, as it was a custom for the firstborn maidens not to leave

the temple without being provided for, it was proper she should be married to whomever it seemed good to them. The high priest obeyed the divine order and, having called together the other priests, he made known to them the will of the Most High. The priests and learned men, moved by divine impulse, concluded that, in a matter where so much was involved and where the Lord Himself had favourably interfered, it would be best to inquire farther into His holy will and to ask Him to designate in some manner who should be the most appropriate person to be the spouse of Mary. Knowing that her spouse must be of the house and of the race of David in order to comply with the law, they appointed a day, on which all the free and unmarried men of that race, who then might be in Jerusalem, were to be called together in the temple. It happened to be the very day on which our princess completed her fourteenth year. As it was necessary to notify her of the result of their conference and to ask her consent, the high priest Simeon called her and informed her of their intention to give her a spouse before dismissing her from the temple.

4. All the selected unmarried men gathered in the temple and prayed to the Lord conjointly with the priests, in order to be governed by the Holy Spirit in what they were about to do. The Most High spoke to the heart of the high priest, inspiring him to place into the hands of each one of the young men a dry branch, with the command that each ask His Majesty with a lively faith, to single out the one whom He had chosen as the spouse of Mary. And as the sweet odour of her virtue and nobility, the fame of her beauty, her possessions and her modesty, and her position as being the

firstborn in her family was known to all of them, each one coveted the happiness of meriting her as a spouse. Among them all only the humble and most upright Joseph thought himself unworthy of such a great blessing; and remembering the vow of chastity which he had made and resolving anew its perpetual observance, he resigned himself to God's will, leaving it all to His disposal and being filled at the same time with a veneration and esteem greater than that of any of the others for the most noble maiden Mary.

5. While they were thus engaged in prayer the branch which Joseph held was seen to blossom and at the same time a dove of purest white and resplendent with admirable light, was seen to descend and rest upon the head of the saint, while in the interior of his heart God spoke, "Joseph, My servant, Mary shall be your spouse; accept her with attentive reverence, for she is acceptable in My eyes, just and most pure in soul and body, and you shall do all that she shall say to you." At this manifestation and token from heaven the priests declared saint Joseph as the spouse selected by God Himself for the maiden Mary. Calling her forth for her espousal, the chosen one issued forth like the sun, more resplendent than the moon, and she entered into the presence of all with a countenance more beautiful than that of an angel, incomparable in the charm of her beauty, nobility and grace; and the priests espoused her to the most chaste and holy of men, saint Joseph.

6. The heavenly princess, more pure than the stars of the firmament, with tearful and sorrowful countenance and as the Queen of majesty, most humble yet uniting all perfections

within herself, took leave of the priests, asking their blessing, and of her instructress and her companions, begging
their pardon. She gave thanks to all of them for the favours
received at their hands during her stay in the temple. The
humility of her behaviour enhanced the prudence and apt-
ness of her words for the performance of these last duties in
the temple; for on all occasions she spoke in few and weighty
words. She took leave of the temple not without great grief
on account of the sacrifice of her inclinations and desires.
In the company of attendants who were some of the more
distinguished laymen in the service of the temple, she betook
herself with her spouse Joseph to Nazareth, the native city
of this most fortunate married couple. Joseph, although
he had been born in that place, had, by the providential
disposition of circumstances, decided to live for some time
in Jerusalem. Thus it happened that he so improved his
fortune as to become the spouse of her, whom God had
chosen to be His own mother.

7. Having arrived at their home in Nazareth, where the
princess of heaven had inherited the possessions and estates
of her blessed parents, saint Joseph said to his spouse Mary,
"My spouse and lady, I give thanks to the Lord most high
God for the favour of having designed me as your husband
without my merits, though I judged myself unworthy even of
your company; I beg of you to supply my deficiencies in the
fulfilment of the domestic duties and of other things, which
as a worthy husband, I should know how to perform; tell
me, lady, what is your pleasure, in order that I may fulfil it."
The heavenly spouse heard these words with a humble heart,
and yet also with a serene earnestness, and she answered the

saint, "I consecrated myself to God by a perpetual vow of chastity in body and soul; His I am and Him I acknowledge as my spouse and Lord, with fixed resolve to preserve for Him my chastity. I beseech you, my master, to help me in fulfilling this vow, while in all other things I will be your servant, willing to work for the comfort of your life as long as mine shall last. Yield, my spouse, to this resolve and make a like resolve, in order that, offering ourselves as an acceptable sacrifice to our eternal God, He may receive us in the odour of sweetness and bestow on us the eternal goods for which we hope." The most chaste spouse Joseph, full of interior joy at the words of His heavenly spouse, answered her, "My mistress, in making known to me your chaste and welcome sentiments, you have delighted my heart. I have not opened my thoughts to you before knowing your own. I also acknowledge myself under greater obligation to the Lord of creation than other men; for very early He has called me by His true enlightenment to love Him with an upright heart; and I desire you to know, lady that at the age of twelve years I also made a promise to serve the Most High in perpetual chastity. On this account I now gladly ratify this vow in order not to impede your own; in the presence of His Majesty I promise to aid you, as far as in me lies, in serving Him and loving Him according to your full desires."

8. By divine operation the two most holy and chaste spouses felt an incomparable joy and consolation. The heavenly princess, as one who is the mistress of all virtues and who in all things pursued the highest perfection of all virtues, lovingly corresponded to the desires of saint Joseph. The Most High

also gave to saint Joseph new-purity and complete command over his natural inclinations, so that without hindrance or any trace of sensual desires, but with admirable and new grace, he might serve his spouse Mary, and in her, execute his will and pleasure. They immediately set about dividing the property inherited from saint Joachim and Ann, the parents of the most holy Virgin; one part they offered to the temple, where she had stayed, another they destined for the poor, and the third was left in the hands of the holy spouse saint Joseph to be disposed of according to his judgment. Our Queen reserved for herself only the privilege of serving him and of attending to the household duties.

9. In his former life saint Joseph had learnt the trade of carpentry, as being a respectable and proper way of earning a living. He was, however, poor in earthly possessions, and so he asked his most holy spouse whether it was agreeable to her that he should continue to exercise his trade for their good, and in order to give alms. The most prudent Virgin approved of this resolve, saying that the Lord did not wish them to be rich, but poor and lovers of the poor, desirous of helping them in as far as their means would allow. Then arose between the two spouses a holy contest, who should obey the other as superior. But she, who among the humble was the most humble, won in this contest of humility; for as the man is the head of the family, she would not permit this natural order to be inverted. She desired in all things to obey her spouse saint Joseph, asking him solely for permission to help the poor, which the saint gladly gave.

10. Soon after most holy Mary had a vision of the Lord, in which God spoke to her, "My most beloved spouse and chosen one, behold how faithful I am to My promises with those who love Me. Correspond therefore now to My fidelity by observing all the laws of a spouse, in holiness, purity and all perfection and let the company of My servant Joseph, whom I have given You, help you in this task. Obey him as you should and listen to his advice." The most holy Mary responded, "Most high Lord, I praise and magnify You for Your admirable disposition and providence in my regard, though I am so unworthy and poor a creature; I desire to obey You and please You as one having greater obligation to You than any other. Bestow upon me, my Lord, Your divine favour, in order that I may attend to the duties of the state in which You have placed me, never erring from Your commands and wishes. Show me Your good will and blessing and with it I will strive to obey and serve Your servant Joseph as You, my Lord and Maker, command." On such heavenly beginnings was founded the home and the married life of the most holy Mary and saint Joseph. From the eighth of September, when they were espoused, until the twenty-fifth of March following, when the Incarnation of the Divine Word took place, the two spouses thus lived together, being prepared in the meanwhile for the work designated for them by the Most High.

GLORY BE TO THE FATHER   Glory be to the Father, and to the Son, and to the Holy Spirit, as it was in the beginning, is now and ever shall be, world without end. Amen.

THE FATIMA PRAYER O my Jesus, forgive us our sins, save us from the fires of hell, lead all souls to heaven, especially those in most need of Thy mercy.

CONCLUDING PRAYERS *Upon completing the recitation of the Holy Rosary, the following prayers are customary, but others too may be added according to one's devotion and preference.*

HAIL HOLY QUEEN Hail Holy Queen, mother of Mercy, hail our life, our sweetness and our hope. To thee do we cry, poor banished children of Eve, to thee do we send up our sighs, mourning and weeping in this vale of tears. Turn then, most gracious advocate, thine eyes of mercy towards us, and after this, our exile, show unto us the blessed fruit of thy womb, Jesus. O clement, O loving, O sweet Virgin Mary. Pray for us O holy mother of God, that we may be made worthy of the promises of Christ.

Let Us Pray O God, Whose only begotten son, by His life, death and resurrection, has purchased for us the rewards of eternal life, grant we beseech Thee, that meditating on these mysteries of the most Holy Rosary of the Blessed Virgin Mary, we may both imitate what they contain and obtain what they promise, through the same Christ our Lord. Amen.

PRAYER TO SAINT MICHAEL THE ARCHANGEL Holy Michael, Archangel, defend us in the day of battle. Be our safeguard against the wickedness and snares of the devil. May God rebuke him, we humbly pray; and do thou, O Prince of the heavenly hosts, by the power of God thrust down

into hell Satan and all the evil spirits who wander through the world seeking the ruin of souls. Amen.

MEMORARE   Remember, O most gracious Virgin Mary, that never was it known that anyone who fled to thy protection, implored thy help, or sought thine intercession was left unaided. Inspired by this confidence, I fly unto thee, O Virgin of virgins, my mother; to thee do I come, before you I stand, sinful and sorrowful. O mother of the Word Incarnate, despise not my petitions, but in thy mercy hear and answer me. Amen.

May the Divine Assistance remain always with us, and may the souls of the faithful departed, through the mercy of God rest in peace. Amen.

Printed in Great Britain
by Amazon